Italian Hillb

"An Italian hillbilly?" you might ask,
"What exactly could that be?"
Well, he's raised in Appalachia
His ancestors came from over the sea.

He's a mixture of two cultures
Separate, but somehow intertwined,
To be a West Virginian
He's now happily resigned.

He goes down into the mines to work
Each and every day without fail.
And you just might find a pepperoni role
Or two, in his dinner pail.

He's a Jerry West fan
And drives a pickup truck;
He can shoot a twenty foot jumper,
Or an eight or ten point buck.

He might drink a glass of Chianti
Along with his corned beef hash.
He listens to Mario Lanza
And sometimes Johnny Cash.

Sunday dinner without pasta
Somehow wouldn't be right.
But it's gotta be southern fried chicken
Nearly every Saturday night.

He's got an Italian heritage

Mixed in with his country ways;
He can whip up some biscuits and gravy
Or baked Ziti with Bolognese.

He's a mountaineer, Italian style;
He stands up straight and tall.
Plants Pomodora Roma in the springtime
And goes deer huntin' in the fall.

Don't criticize his mixed up ways
That's the only rule.
'Cause cornbread goes just dandy, thanks-
With a bowl of pasta faziole.

He's proud to be American,
And he'll quickly tell you why.
And you bet he flies the stars and stripes
And not just on the fourth of July.

His grandpa came from Calabria
Back a hundred years or so.
And when Uncle Sam comes callin'
He'll be the first to go.

He was on the beach in Normandy
In Viet Nam a ranger man.
In the deserts of the Middle East
Or the mountains of Afghanistan/

For first he is a patriot
Of that you may have no fear.
He's one hell of a combination-
A Mediterranean Mountaineer.

Ravioli
and
Rhododendron

A Collection of Childhood Memories

of an Italian Hillbilly

by

TOM OLIVETO

Italian Hillbilly Publishing, LLC

Ravioli and Rhododendron

ISBN:978-0-9984374-0-8
ISBN(E book) 978-0-9984374-1-5

Published by Italian Hillbilly Publishing, LLC, Pompano Beach, FL
www.italianhillbilly.com
First Publication: November, 2016

Printed in the United States of America

For my parents,

Thomas Oliveto, Sr. and Rosina B. Oliveto

Acknowledgements

I would like to express my appreciation to the following individuals who played a part in the production of this book, and/or in the production of the memories of my early years which inspired it:

To my sister, Barbara O. Joyce, for the sixty-odd years of shared memories.

To my Nana, Teresa Barberio, for her unconditional love.

To my Nanu, Frank Barberio and my Grandpa and Grandma, John and Barbara Oliveto, for their dedication to hard work and family values.

To all my Aunts and Uncles, who served as a secondary set of parents when needed.

To my cousins, for all the memories. In an Italian family, cousins are not distant relatives, but more like brothers and sisters. So I thank you all: Mickey, Dyane, Louis Thomas, Charlene, John Francis D., John Francis B., Frank Joseph, and Stephen Paul. To Barbara Lynn, Anthony, Guy Thomas, John B., Judy Ann, Larry, Gina, Jimmy Joe, John O., Sam, Barbara, Tom, and Joey.

To my nephews, Joe, John, Tom, and Tim, for continuing on with many of our family's traditions.

To my gang of listeners: Joe J., Sandy, Debi, Manohara, Stephanie, Dave, Lori, Judy W., Judy S., Lisa, John G., and Jamie.

To Cheryl, for having the good grace to laugh at all my attempts at humor, no matter how feeble they may be.

To Max, whose "two cents" is always worth at least a dime.

To Solina, for her hard work and dedication, particularly in post-production, without whom the completion of this "project" would not have been possible. And

To Ulli, for her kind words of encouragement.

Thank you all.

Contents

Contents (Cont.)

Foreword

When they think of the state of West Virginia, most Americans who have never been there think of coal mines, poverty, and perhaps moonshiners. Those who have actually had the need to drive through the state, usually to get to some destination in the South, will be reminded of winding two-lane country roads and deep green tree-covered hills. If they were lucky enough to take that trip in the fall, they will no doubt remember the beautiful scenery afforded by the colors of the changing foliage—the brilliant reds and golds of autumn in the Mountain State.

Yes, there are a lot of coal mines (many fewer than there once were). A few folks still make moonshine, but it is not nearly as common as it was in the past, and the average resident could live their entire lives in the state without ever directly encountering it. And yes, there is some poverty, but not as much as you might think. The stereotype of poverty in Appalachia is the exception, not the norm. The barefooted family living in a wooden shack up in the "hollers" can still be found, but even these people have a wealth that cannot be measured in dollars and cents. It is a wealth of heritage—a wealth of tradition.

Everyone from West Virginia who has traveled even minimally outside the state knows only too well that the average American knows little or nothing about the state, and many, in fact, do not even know that it is a separate state from Virginia, U.S. geography not being a particularly strong suit of our educational system. The reality is that the two states are about as much alike as are Pennsylvania and Mississippi.

Carved out of the western half of Virginia during the Civil War, the history, geography, and demographics of West Virginia is quite unique. In my own travels around the country, most people I meet are surprised that there is a man with an Italian last name who is from West Virginia.

"How did the Italians get there?" one might ask. A Michigan native recently told me that he would have expected a predominantly WASPish population in the state. This is easily understandable, given the typical settlement of the American Frontier. But things began to change in the middle of the 1800's in West Virginia.

A lot of Germans, Austrians, Belgians, and French came to work in the burgeoning glass industry. The Irish were no doubt drawn to the fact that the green hills reminded them of their native land. And the booming coal mining industry, which required a lot of both skilled and manual labor, afforded opportunities to immigrants of steady work. In the late 1800's, this included not only the aforementioned groups, but also the Scottish, Spanish, Polish, and Italians. After New York City had reached its saturation point of Italian carpenters, bricklayers, and stonemasons, the rest came to Pennsylvania and West Virginia to work in the coal mines, glass factories, and the new chemical plants in the Kanawha Valley.

Consequently, there are a lot of West Virginians of Italian descent, and this book is about those people. It is not, however, intended to be an accurate historical account of the Italian immigrant in the Mountain State. Nor does it in any way attempt to recount the experience of an entire group of people. Italians are a very diverse group. So, too, are West Virginia Mountaineers. It is merely a hodge-podge of memories of one young child born a half century after the Italians came to settle in Central West Virginia. A child who was often confused by the culture clash of a largely old-world based family in a unique American environment. A child who, at the time of his upbringing, was not even remotely aware of his tremendous good fortune, namely that of being an "Italian Hillbilly."

Occio Russo

The following is a mostly true account of a small part of the childhood of one Tommy Oliveto, age four.

'Twas the night before Christmas
and all through the town
the shoppers were bustling
up Main Street and down.

And Pike Street as well
was full of good cheer,
save the occasional drunk
who'd had too much beer.

A safe place to go
was our little town,
Main Street going up
Pike coming back down.

But where the two came together
at the old Angle Inn
'Twas there that dwelt something
As evil as sin.

Don't look up child!
And walk fast and loose,
Lest you're caught in the gaze
Of old Occio Russo *

Yes indeed — Clarksburg, West Virginia was a safe and pleasant place to grow up, and very little that was bad or upsetting ever came into the lives of the two little kids that lived in the two hundred block of Milford Street in Stealey. And I don't know how the legend of the big red eye man was originally hatched, but it must have been a ruse to scare the hell out of small children who didn't behave.

Now Barbara and I were never whipped of mistreated, and were never (to my memory) threatened with the boogie man or the big bad wolf. However, it was made painfully clear often and with gusto that if you didn't behave the big red one was gonna getcha.

Now in the daytime, the monster was completely harmless, and was, in reality, a large red oval beer sign (Falls City Beer, to be exact) which stood at Angle Inn, the intersection of Pike Street and Main. Why it was called Angel Inn I have no idea, since there was no Inn anywhere around, but it was, in fact, sort of an angle, since the two streets which were actually parallel to each other suddenly just sort of ran together at a sharp angle.

And from its perch at the top of a small triangular building, the Falls City Beer Sign could see nearly everything from Pierpont School to the top of Stealey Hill and beyond. It was indeed master of all it surveyed, and all day long would just sit there glistening in the sun, extolling the benefits of a tall, cool frosty Falls City. Well, as I said, in the daytime it was completely harmless, and the worst that could be said was that it was a bit tacky, being that

3

gawdy red color and all, and sort of faded and in need of a new coat of paint nearly all the time. I wasn't afraid of it one bit and would walk right by it (holding on to Barbara's hand, or my mother's hand, or Zizi Marguerite's hand or Zizi Buckie's hand or Zizi Thelma's hand, or Dear God, whoever's hand happened to be, well, handy. And in the daytime you could just look right at it with no consequences whatsoever. But when the sun set, the neon tubes that outlined the words and the border would be ignited, and the big red sign took on the appearance of this huge bloodshot eye and stared out at everything it could see. Yes, come darkness and the tacky but innocuous commercial advertisement became "he who sees all", "he who cannot be deceived," "he who knows all you are thinking and all the mischief you have ever done, or even thought about doing," "the evil one", "the one whose name you dare not speak".....the Occio Russo.

Again, I don't know exactly whose sick little mind came up with the idea of scaring my sister and I with the concept of an all-seeing, all-knowing, big red eye monster to keep us in line, but I can say that it must have worked, since we were both very well behaved most of the time. I guess it's a part of raising children that you need to have something to scare the crap out of them, and it is a real art to come up with something that is scary enough to do the trick, and if you happen to screw up their little minds for the rest of their life, well, so be it. We all have to be maladjusted in one way or another. And this was, after all, 1955. Hitler was long since dead and buried in a pile of rubble, Osama Bin Laden had not yet come along, Khrushchevjust wasn't scary enough, and even I knew the big bad wolf was only a fairy tale. The best thing we had to frighten the kiddies in

4

the late fifties was Fidel Castro, and to me he looked too much like Doug Windon, the nice man down at the tire store, to be at all scary. And so, it must have been necessary to invent a red eye man to keep us in line. Fidel and his missiles in Cuba were a bit too high tech and misunderstood to work on a four-year-old. After all, in Mrs. Pinnell's kindergarten class we had been practicing the old "Duck and Cover" and had become quite adept at jumping under our desks in the event of an attack. My thoughts, as I recall, at the time were "Sure, Okay, hiding under this little pine desk is fine for a thermonuclear warhead, but what do you have for a real threat, like Occio Russo?"

One thing which was not quite clear to me, however, was exactly what was he going to do to you if he gotcha? Would he eat you, or just squash you like a bug, or what? I decided that all he had to do was just sort of stare at you with that big red eyeball and that would be enough.

And where did he come from ? The other little kids in kindergarten had never heard of him, which I thought was kind of strange because they could see him plain as day right up on top of that building down the street. I decided that he must be Italian, since he had an Italian name and all, so I figured he must have come over on the boat with the rest of the old folks. Could you just picture him arriving at Ellis Island, and applying for a visa? Name? Occio Russo. Occupation? Terrorizer of small children. Do you have any special skills? I can stare at kids and tell if they've been bad or not. Okay, Mr Russo, here's a visa, now go to Clarksburg, West Virginia and keep an eye on those kids in Stealey.

5

Even in church you weren't quite safe. I remember one time during my first year of catechism, in studying for our first Holy Communion, Sister Mary Bob (That was one of the nuns who taught us bible study) asked me if I was afraid of Satan. Now I knew that she was always trying to trip you up, so she could make her point; that was her way, even though she was a very good teacher and always nice to us kids—that's why we called her Sister Mary Bob; that was my idea. You see her real name was Sister Mary Robert, and since we liked her and all, and all us kids had a nickname—I was Tommy, Dominick Bacardi was Nicky, and Vincent Giasullo was Vinnie. It was my idea to call her Sister Mary Bob since I knew that Bob was a nickname for Robert— well, that's how I remember it, but Nicky Bacardi would probably tell you that is was because she had this funny way of walking which made her head go up and down, sort of "bob", you know; well she always looked sort of like a penguin pecking at the ground. But I digress—anyway Sister Mary Bob asked me if I'm afraid of Satan and I say

"No, sister, I'm not." To which she replies,

"That's good, Tommy, but why not?" And I say

"Because Jesus is with me every where I go." I had read the lesson like I was supposed to. So Sister Mary Bob says ,

"So then you're not afraid of anything, right?"

Well I wasn't quite sure of whether lying to a nun was a

mortal or venial sin, so I figured to be on the safe side I'd better tell the truth so I said,

"Well, I'm a little bit afraid of Occio Russo."
I can see she doesn't quite understand, not being Italian probably, and is questioning me when Vinnie pipes up and says,

"I'm afraid of him too, sister."

Since I had told Nicky and Vinnie the Occio Russo story, and Dominick thinks I'm full of crap and he's not afraid of no beer sign, him being nearly six and all, but when I told Vinnie the story, I thought he was gonna fill up his pants right on the spot, and he says he ain't never goin' to Stealey for as long as he lives.

Well, just about then Father Bandiera stops by to check in on the class and I hear Sister Mary Bob ask him what " Occio Russo" means, and he says,

"Oh it means red eye. It's probably another version of the Evil Eye, an old superstition," and tells us that it isn't real and we don't have to be afraid if it.   So here I am thinking,

"Yeah, well, he may be a Priest and all, and over six feet tall and everything, but I bet if I take him down to Angle Inn some night after sunset, he will wish he was at Lourdes or something. After all, I had told the truth. I wasn't afraid of the devil and if I ever saw him I would tweak his horns and pull his pointy tail, and kick him square in his little red ass, but Occio Russo was an eye of a different color altogether. He was the "maloiche", the "zingada" and the "atziata" all rolled into one.

After all, my Nana had told me about him, and my Nana doesn't lie. Here is a woman who can make you a meatball as big as my punkin' head and can stir her coffee without moving her fingers. You try that. Not many people can do it. It's a regular gift directly from God, I tell you, and if my Nana says the beer sign is a monster, then you can take it to the bank and earn interest. And, I for one , am not going to get on the bad side of you know who.

Now I figure that if he had to, Occio Russo could whip both the devil and Bruno Sammartino at the same time on Studio Wrestling, if he wanted to, and I don't know where he stands on the "who's badder" list with Jesus, because our Bible study book seems to be silent on the subject. So I figure the smart four-year-old will take no chances, walking with Jesus or not. I figure Jesus will understand, besides for all I know Jesus may be afraid of him too. Probably not, but why take the chance?

By this time I had made up my own set of rules where childhood monsters were concerned. The aforementioned bag bad wolf did not exist, the thing that lived under my bed couldn't get you as long as you didn't dangle your feet over the edge, and the boogieman—well what was that anyway, a man with an excess buildup of nasal mucus? Sounds more repulsive than scary. And the devil, well, all the pictures I'd ever seen of him sort of reminded me of my Uncle Tony, with those pointy little features and all, and I liked my Uncle Tony—he could pull a quarter out from behind your ear and give it to you—doesn't seem like an evil trick to me—you got to keep the quarter.

And so it was with Occio Russo. You had to know the rules and then you would be Okay.

Rule #1 – Daytime-no problem
Rule #2 – Behind the sign-nothing to fear; he can't see you back there.
Rule #3 – If you can see him, he can see you. If you can't see him, he can't see you.
Rule #4 – More powerful in winter than in summer. In summer he was partially hidden by the trees, but when the leaves fell, look out! I used to cuss out the Monongahela Power trucks when they trimmed the trees in the summer, because he could see you better. But you had to forgive
them; I don't think they were aware of the em problem.
Rule #5 — And this one always confused me— Occio Russo is only a threat to small children. Adults do not appear to be afraid of him in the least. Nana and Zizi's would always say "He's gonna get you if you're not good!" Never "he's gonna get *us!*", just "*you!*"

Now I used to think my Zizi Buckie was so brave, because lots of times she would walk home from her job at the telephone company, and she would just march right on by Angle Inn without so much as a "howja do?" And Zizi Thelma would get this sort of funny grin on her face whenever the evil one was mentioned-she wasn't afraid either. Now Zizi Marguerite would make a big deal of it and say,

"OOOH yeah boy, You better be good." She would act like she was afraid of it too, for our benefit, of course, to heighten the effect. As a matter of fact, if I had to lay odds as to who it was who came up with the idea in the first place—well, I better not. I don't know so I won't say. Still....

Now in the summertime, when the Conley's came to visit, I remember one time when Zizi Michaelena told me she wasn't afraid of anything—-not even snakes (which was baloney). So I said,

"Not even Occio Russo?"

The next thing you know Zizi Mike is storming into the kitchen demanding to know,

"Now which one of my genius sisters has taught this boy to be afraid of a beer sign?" After discussing it with my Zizi Ray (He was at first reluctant to meddle in what must have seemed a family affair to him) we decided that the beer sign was probably just about as powerful at night as it was in the daytime. Except it was lit up. By something called *Neon*. I figured that's where the power came from. Neon must be like Krypton, except probably stronger. My cousin Mickey said she wasn't afraid either.

"Easy for you to say," I remember thinking "Occio Russo doesn't live in Georgia, or Japan dammit, that's out of his jurisdiction. He can't see *you*. He lives here—right down the street. I'm not afraid of Bigfoot, either—I don't have to walk past the Himalayas. And I'm not afraid of Godzilla, either, but if I were you, when you get back to Japan, I wouldn't go strolling on the beach alone." Come to find out, Mickey said she was afraid too, when she was little. So I figured I would be afraid of Occio Russo until my hand could fill out the impression of Mickey's in the cement outside Nana's back door. But until then I would watch my P's and Q's just to be on the safe side.

Now the really confusing one was Nana. I think it was she who first told us about Occio Russo, but she didn't seem to be in too much awe at the sight of him, I can picture a scene even now—I'm out in Nana's back yard playing at something. It is about sundown. Nana appears on the back stoop, probably with something for me to eat, and suddenly proclaims in a sing-song matter-of-fact tone:

"Chickie! Vuarda! E benuto Occio Russo!" Like she's just noticed an old friend has dropped by for Sunday dinner.

"Look, Mary and Teddy are here! Well well, Millie Minger's here. Come in and have a piece of cobbler! Chickie! E benuto Occio Russo!"

So here's the scene: Mickey, Barbara and I are outside on a warm summer evening. We've all got maynoaise jars and we're collecting lightening bugs (Firelies to you non-hillbillies). Maybe Tommy Diaz is there. And Maybe Dyane. Butchie and John Francis are too little. Charlene is almost old enough but wouldn't touch a bug on her life. Frank and Stephen are not even around yet. I know the rules-I'm around the side of the house by the garage. I tell the others that I'm over there because the lightning bugs go for the big hydrangea bush by the driveway. But I'm no dummy- I know that the sun has set, and soon the Krypton-Neon powered big red eye is about to become... you guessed it— OCCIO RUSSO!

Or here's another scenario: It's early on a midsummer evening. We've had dinner. Maybe Daddy is working late. Mom is going to take Barb and I down to the West End to the Dairy Queen for a treat. Hot dang! Now this is just about as good as it gets! The whole trip is a fantastic voyage for a four-year-old. And it ends up right at the Dairy Queen—my favorite place in the whole world, or at least in what I know of the world. Dairy Queen—home of the curly-top cone, the Mr. Misty, and the piece de resistance, the hot fudge sundae. Could there be anything better than a hot fudge sundae? I would do anyting for a hot fudge sundae. I would lie to a nun—no, two-nuns. I would lie to two nuns standing together for a hot fudge sundae. And the trip itself is a treat.

First we get to cross Fairview Avenue—this huge street that goes all the way down and turns into a big circle—how neat is that? And in the middle of the circle is this huge pine tree that they put lights on at Christmas. And after Fairview Avenue we go past the Apartments which is this unbelievably huge building that must be two or three hundred storied tall. I figure it's probably about as big as the Umpire State Building on TV. And it takes a long time to walk all the way past it, and then there is the tire store where Mr. Windon fixes the tires. Of course, it's after closing, and we don't get to see him, which is a real shame because he is a lot of fun to watch because he gets to get real dirty and nobody cares. Sometimes he gets so dirty that he's almost black, and he looks like Julius the janitor at the kindergarten. But Julius isn't dirty, he's just that color. Then we come to the West End Motors, which is a car dealership, and all the new Mercurys are lined up in the lot right by the street and I have to touch all of them on the fender as we pass. It's a ritual sort of thing. But I have to remember to pick up some rocks from the gravel lot because the river is coming up next. I will have to pester Mom to hold me up so that I can see over the wall to throw the rocks (one at a time) into the river. Now if anyone here can't rmember just how cool it is to throw rocks into a river, then I feel sorry for you because you are just plain old. Now you would think that so far this is just exciting enough to satisfy a four-year-old, and by golly, don't you think it oughta be, but there's more to come. After the river we get to cross the railroad tracks by the Purina Store. And the Purina Store smells like animals or something, which is really neat, too. And then (and this you just will not believe) we walk right in front of the Fire Station and there are always two firemen sitting outside in folding chairs in front of what has to be the biggest, shiniest fire truck you have ever seen. Now I'm pretty tall for four, but I barely come up to the hubcaps on this mother. The firemen always say hello 'cause they know us, and that is neat to know that really important people like firemen know who we are and stuff.

Finally we are almost there, and all we have to do is cross the big street and there is the Dairy Queen. The trip to the Dairy Queen is about the greatest thing that can happen, but as is always the case in life, it carries a big price. For there at the end of the street, looking right down on us, and I mean RIGHT down on us is you-know-who in all his glory.

His view of us is completely unobstructed, and it surely must be getting close to sunset, since we've had dinner already. Well, it shouldn't be a problem-after all, how long could it take to go across the street, get our treats, and start back home? Just a couple minutes probably. We're waiting for the traffic to clear so we can cross, when this big old station wagon pulls up next to the Dairy Queen and this big fat lady and about a zillion kids get out. Oh No! Thery're getting in line in front of us. No way we can beat them to the window; we have to wait to cross the street!

Well, finally we get behind them and they are taking forever to get their act together. This whole brood of barefoot dirty kids and Fat Momma are gonna take forever. They are all talking at once and yelling,

"I want this" and "I want that"! Here I am thinking this bunch of farnistu's is gonna take forever and the sun is getting ready to set and the Neon is gonna come on and here we are right out in the open and what's taking so long, and I bet these people are from Mount Clare 'cause I heard somebody say that once. And the littlest kid of them al can't make up his mind and Fat Momma is saying

"Now tell the lady what flavor milkshake you want, Bobby," and he can't decide and the sun is getting lower in the sky and everything, and I'm about ready to shout,

"Make up your damn mind, Bobby! For cryin' out loud this is Dairy Queen, 1955—there are only two damn flavors—it ain't Baskin Robbins, ya know! You're gonna get us all killed!"

So, after about a hunded hours, the Beaver decides on a
chocolate shake, which I couldda told ya that in the first
place, and the lady starts to makin up the treats and Bobby's
bawlin' again because some of the other kids are already
eating their ice cream cause they didn't take a year to
decide, and Fat Momma is yelling at him to shut up and is
threatening him with not getting to go to the carnival which
is apparently why they are in town in the first place, and the
sun is clear down over the roof on the Canteen already, and
I'm thinking we're all about to be fried like a dozen eggs
and she's threatening him with the carnival, and I would
like to tell him what the real danger is—right up the street,
but I figure Mom would tell me that that's not polite and
I'm thinking my last few minutes on earth are being held up
to the scrutiny of etiquette. I decide I better see what time
it is and I look at my wrist and Damn! I forgot to wind my
Roy Rogers watch and the big hand is just sitting there on
Trigger's nose and it ain't even moving! So I look around
for a clock to set it by, because I know how to do that, even
though I'm only four, and for weeks now, I have been going
around setting clocks all over the place, even the ones that
were already set, and Nana even climbed on a chair to get
the one down over the sink so that I could set it because it
was five minutes fast and then everybody was late for
something because they all knew it was five minutes fast,
and took that into account and, Damn! I can hardly not
even see the sun behind the roof of the Canteen and Oh!
There's a clock on the wall inside the Dairy Queen, and
now I can set my watch, but the clock on the wall says two-
thirty and I know it ain't no two-thirty because we've
already had dinner and Mom wouldn't let us be eatin' ice
cream before dinner. And I notice that the electric cord
coming out of the clock is just dangling there and it ain't

15

plugged in to nothing and the blue light outside the store that zaps the bugs has just come on and if it is set to come on now, then can the evil one be far behind?

So Mom asks me if I have to go to the bathroom, and I say,
"No, why? And Barb says,

"Oh, Mother, he's just fidgeting—you know how he fidgets." And I'm thinking,

"Yeah, easy for you to say," and I figure maybe Barbara isn't even afraid of Occio Russo anymore cause she's like, seven already, and finally, finally, the lady brings Beaver his milkshake and they are on their way and Mom is saying,

"Tell the lady what you want", and we do, and I decided on a Mr. Misty because they have this new blue flavor, and I never had that before and it looks kinda neat, sorta like bright blue Play-Dough. Just when I think we are making some progress the lady disappears into the back of the store to get something. I can't imagine what, and Mom and Barb are cool as a couple of cucumbers and I'm thinking,

"Don't they know what's at stake here?" The sun is now all the way past the roof on the Canteen and the bug zapper just fries a June bug or something and, "What the *hell* are you making back there lady, a damn Teiela?"

Just then another bug lights up the zapper, and I'm thinking that's what's gonna happen to us if this lady doesn't "get the rag out" like Zizi Marguerite says, when she comes

16

back with the biggest milk carton thing I ever saw and pours the stuff into the top of the machine. So now we're cookin with gas, and we get our stuff and Mom pays the lady and we are now ready to cross the street and we'll be around the bend (where he can't see us) in no time. Well, we're holding Mom's hand which she insists on when we cross a street, and we're waiting for traffic to clear, and I'm slurping on the Mr. Misty which tastes like nothing in particular, and I'm thinkin',

"Maybe shoulda stuck with the hot fudge sundae, but then it's hot out and when it's hot outside the thing just melts into a big gooey mess before you can eat it, and I'm probably better off because at least the blue thing doesn't change halfway through." When all of a sudden I'm reminded of the fact that Mom will not cross the street with us if there is a car anywhere in sight, and I'm sayin',

"Mom I could run across this street six times before that car gets here." And she, of course answers with:

"Sometimes they are going faster than they look, or you could trip and fall or ….…." so I respond with,

"But Mom, he's not even coming here, he's turning into the Hartland Planing Mill and he's so far away and …"

And nothing—I know better. We will cross the street only when there are no cars at all between here and Bridgeport, and tomorrow when we go to the pool I will have to stay out of the pool for at least an hour after eating a pack of Nabs or something, so I won't get a cramp and sink to the bottom of the pool like a little rock. And I'm thinking Mom is over cautious. But then why are we dawdling at the side of the street while the real danger is probably only seconds away from getting the juice that runs the Neon or Krypton, or whatever and.....

"Okay. Let's go!" Mom says and we're crossing the street, with Barb on one side of Mom and me on the other. And we reach the other side, and start back towards home. Only maybe a hundred yards or so and we will be around the bend and out of sight of Ol' Falls City Slim, and I swear I can feel his gaze on the back of my neck as we walk …. almost past the firehouse now—good thing too, 'cause the shadows are pretty long and a car passed with his parking lights on, which means...and Yow! I feel this terrific pain in the back of my head and I'm thinking,

"This is it—the jig is up! I'm a goner and I'm gonna croak right there on the sidewalk and I ain't never even started school yet, and I hope Bobby throws up his chocolate shake all over himself at the carnival, and what the hell *is* a carnival anyway, and here I 'm gonna die before I ever saw a carnival, and the *pain!*." And I turn around to look, thinkin', "what the hell, can't hurt— I'm dead anyway", and I look up at the sign and it ain't even lit yet, but how come the pain and...

And that was how I learned that if a thirty-five pound boy tries to drink a ten ounce Mr. Misty in under a minute, his head is gonna hurt something fierce.

So, almost home now and,

"Hey look, there's a black car pulling into Fairview. Looks like Dad's home!" So Mom lets go of my hand and I run to tell Dad that we threw rocks into the river, and crossed the tracks and saw the Fire Truck, and the new Merc's are in and there's a Mr Misty now which is actually blue, and I'm feeling really cool 'cause I got on my PF Flyers and my Xavier Cougat shirt. And I'm a big boy now and I ain't afraid of no beer sign, neither.

And so I lived to tell about it, and the next year I went to school and coming home down Duff Street every afternoon, I could climb up on the wall and from there you could see the sign and I would laugh to think how silly it was to be afraid of anything, and a few years later somebody named Mr. Johnny Smallwood came to town to save all the little kids in Stealey from the monster. You see he bought the little triangular building, tore down the old sign and put up a bright new one. It was green and white and had friendly little shamrocks on it and it read:

John Smallwood
Insurance
Home, Life, Auto, Causality

Not enough to scare anybody. So it just goes to show you-what can scare you when you're little just builds character. And it just might make you behave and mind your parents. Worked for us. And I don't seem to be any the worse for wear about it, either. One thing however— To this day I can't bring myself to order a Falls City. No great loss, anyway—the stuff tastes like crap. And besides, a Hieneken can't stare you down until you shrivel up and die. And a Miller Lite not only tastes great, but it's less filling, and it can't look down into you and rip out your soul

19

and wring it out like an old dishrag. Well, you get the picture.

And I can't wait to see Michael, so that I can tell him this:
In three more years you're going to be four. And four kinda sucks. You're just old enough to know a thing or two, but too little to do anything about it. And people will try to feed you a line of horsepucky every now and then. But don't worry, four only last a year, and that's not very long. Now your old Uncle Tom would never steer you wrong. He might lie to a nun or two, but not to you. Just remember—
There is no boogie man. There is no big bad wolf. There's nothing that lives under your bed except maybe a few dust mites and they're so small you can't even see 'em. And I am happy to report that there is no Occio Russo.

The lady behind the counter of the State Department of Motor Vehicles, however, is very real. So is the IRS. So just renew your license by mail early, never fill out a W-4 form, don't give anyone your correct social security number, and always give a discount for anyone paying cash. If they can't see you, they can't get you.

> And he said to them all
> As he flew out of sight
> Merry Christmas to all!
> And stay out of the light!*

---

* Adapted from 'Twas The Night Before Christmas by Clement Clarke Moore

Saint John the Baptist

So I'm sitting in church one Sunday fidgeting around in the pew like a typical seven-year-old, totally bored by Father Bandiera's homily- in which he's going over the calendar of upcoming events. He is reminding the congregation of next Saturday's bake sale over at another church— "Our Lady of the Bleeding Spleen" (or whatever), and I happen to notice that all of the missals in the rack in front of me have been stamped on the back cover "Property of Saint John the Baptist Holy Roman Catholic Church". And I start to wonder (not for the first time) why our church is called that.

So I decide after church I'm going to ask Mom- she'll know. Sometimes she explains things right off, but sometimes she says,

"Why don't you go look it up? You'll remember it longer." To which my first reply is,

"Oh Mom, can't you just tell me? I'll remember—I promise." But I know I'm going to have to go check the encyclopedia or that damn unabridged (whatever *that* means) dictionary that sits on that little table in the family room.

That thing was about as big as I was and was considerably heavier. Mom got it at the supermarket in one of those buy-a-chapter-a-week deals, and you want to look up "monkey" but "M" doesn't arrive 'till next week, so you settle for "lemur" which came yesterday, and finally after twenty-six weeks you have a book for which you just might have to put an addition on the house to accommodate.

So the question then becomes "will Mom just cave and tell me or am I going to have to go look it up?" And if it's the latter, the next question is "do I really need to know this or is it easier to just remain stupid." But I decide that in this case the origin of the name of just one church among thousands is not likely to be in the *World Book*, so it's probably safe to hit Mom up with this one.

After Mass, Mom and I are sitting at the kitchen table, she with her newspaper and me with the comics, just killing some time before it's time to go up to Nana's house for Sunday dinner with the whole family. This would be a good time to ask her about the name of the church.

"Hey Mom, I noticed that all of the missals in church have the name of the church stamped on the back of them."

Mom: "Uh huh."

"And, oh yeah— Mrs. Thomas says they're going to shoot a missal up into space this week— why would they shoot a missal up into space?"

"That's not a missal" (and she spells it). " That's a missile" (and she spells that too, like that is going to help).

"So Mom, are we Baptist or are we Catholic? Or are we Baptist Catholic?"

"We are Catholic."

"So then why is our church called *Saint John the Baptist Holy Roman Catholic Church?*"

"Saint John was the Baptist."

"But why would we name our church after a Baptist if we are Catholic?'

"Saint John wasn't *a* Baptist, he was *the* Baptist. He was the one who Baptized people. There were actually several Saint Johns."

"Yeah. In catechism class we learned about *Saint John the Regulator.*"

Mom (laughing): "I think you mean *Saint John the Revelator.* That was Saint John, the Apostle."

"What's a revelator?"

Mom: "Like the Book of Revelations."

"So he was a guy who revelates?"

"*Reveals* is the word you're looking for."

"What did he reveal?"

"He was the one who revealed God's plan. And the end of days, the Apocalypse. God came to him in a vision."

"So this guy John, who saw the apple eclipse, wasn't John the Baptist?"

Mom: "No, he was John the Apostle. He was one of the twelve. You know about the twelve."

"Yeah. The Twelve signs of the Kodiak. Like me- I'm a Taurus."

Mom: " Not Kodiak, the *Zodiak*. A Kodiak is a big bear. And yes, you are a Taurus. Boy are you *ever* a Taurus. If there ever was a Taurus that would be you. I should have let Dr. Marks induce labor like he wanted to—then you would have been an Aries and we would probably not be having this particular conversation."
I didn't know what she meant by that, but I took it as a good thing and an invitation to continue.

Me: " Yeah, the Big Bear. It's one of the consolations."

Mom: "Constellations. Yes, the Big Bear *is* one of the constellations. There's Ursa Major, the big bear, and there's a little bear, too. Ursa Minor."

Me: "I saw that on the map in Mrs. Mathews' geography class. It's where Turkey is."

"That's *Asia* Minor. But anyway, the "Twelve" we're talking about are the twelve Apostles, and one of them was John. John the Apostle."

"But he was also John the Revelator."

"That's right. And there were other Saint Johns. I think there was one who was called *John the Evangelist.*"

"So the one who was called John the Baptist, was he a catholic?"

Mom: "Roman Catholic."

"Saint John was Roman?"

"No, of course not."

Me: "But he was Catholic, right?"

Mom: "Well…no, not yet, but he was a Christian."

"Saint John the Baptist was a Christian?"

Mom: "Yes."

Me: "So there's this guy John, who was a Christian. And he was probably born a Christian because his parents were Christian?"

"No, he was born a Jew."

"He was born a Jew?" And about now I'm starting to think I have been dropped down in between Abbott and Costello doing a performance of *Who's on First?*.

"Yes. His parents were Jewish and he was born a Jew. All the Apostles and such were Jewish at first."

"So he's born a Jew and became a Christian later?"

"Yes."

"So why was he called the 'Baptist'?"

"Because he baptized people into the faith."

Me: "So a baptist is a person who baptizes people?"

"Yes, that's right."

"So my friend Billy Walker baptizes people?"

"Of course not, silly, he's only seven years old."

"But he told me he was a Baptist."

Mom: "He and his family are members of the First Baptist Church, so that makes him a Baptist. They've all been Baptized. You were Baptized when you were born. Do you remember that Baptismal gown I showed you in the trunk up in the attic? That's what you wore on the day you were Baptized."

"Yeah, but I don't remember being Baptized."

"Of course you don't remember, but you *were* Baptized."

"So how come I'm not a Baptist?"

Mom: "Because you were Baptized into the Roman Catholic Church.

Me: "I don't understand."

Mom: "Look, Honey, it's like this:" (my mother with the patience of Job- and it's pronounced *Job,* even though it's spelled the same as 'job', like you go to work and have a job, and I don't understand that, either and I'm starting to think there's a lot more that I don't understand than there is stuff that I do understand). "God came to John and told him to go out and baptize people and make them Christians and they would be followers of Jesus Christ— Christians. There are lots of kinds of Christians. There are Baptists and Methodists and Lutherans and Episcopalians. And of course Catholics, like us."

"And Presbadalians? The big brick church?"

"Yes, Presbyterians are Christians, too."

"And Prostitutes?"

"Protestants. Yes, Protestants are Christians, too. All those other groups we said- the Baptists, Methodists, Lutherans, and Presbyterians, are all Protestants."

Now I'm thinking this is all about as clear as sun-baked mud, and Mom being the most well-intentioned glutton for suffering, continues:

"So, there were all these followers of Christ, and some of the most devout later became Saints, and more than one of them were named *John,* and so as not to be confused with one another, they were called *John the Baptist, John the Apostle, John the Evangelist,* and so on. But anyway, there were several Saint Johns, and the one who was called Saint John the Baptist is the one we named our church after, and that's why it's called *Saint John the Baptist Roman Catholic Church.*"

Now you think I would have just let it rest there, but that would be too easy. My poor mother! "So where does the 'Roman' part fit in?"

Mom: That came later. It's called the Roman Catholic Church because Rome adopted Christianity a few hundred years after Christ. That's why the head of the Church is in Rome."

"And Rome is in Italy, right?"

"That's right."

"So are we Roman?"

"No."

"But we're Italian, right?"

"Yes, but it's just our ancestry that's Italian. Your grandparents were born in Italy, but they came to the United States when they were very young."

" So how come it's not the *Italian* Catholic Church? If Rome is in Italy?"

Mom: "There wasn't a country called Italy then. It was just the Roman Empire and it was all over the place. But the head of the church was in the city of Rome. Actually, it was in the Vatican. Where the Pope lives."

Me: "Pope John?"

Mom: "Yes."

"So was he named after John the Baptist?"

Mom: "I don't know- maybe, or it might have been John the Apostle, or somebody else. His given name isn't John. When a Cardinal becomes Pope, he chooses a new name— one of the Saints. Before that his name is just the one he was born with."

"So what was Pope John's name before he was Pope?"
Mom: "I don't remember. Why don't you go look it up?"

Shit. Here it is. And I was so close to the end without having to look something up. I decide to change the subject just a little since Mom probably doesn't think the real name of the Pope is something I need to know.

"Okay, Mom. So all these guys who were first Jews, decided to follow Christ and that's how they became Christians?"

"That's right."

Me: "And John the Baptist went around and Baptized a bunch of Jews and then they were Christians after that."

Mom: "Uh huh."

Me: "And why did he do that?"

"Because God told him to."

"And Jesus was God's Son, right?"

Mom: "That's right. Very good, Tommy, very good."

Me: (Thinking not good enough. Not yet) "So if God wanted all these people to follow Christ and become Christians, why did he make his Son be born a Jew?"

Mom (sighing heavily now, the stress starting to show on her poor face): "I'm not sure. Maybe because they were His chosen people. It says that in the Bible."

Me (having a sudden epiphany): "Yeah! They were his chosen people! We read that in the old tenement!"

Mom: "Testament."

Me: "Yeah! They were his chosen people. But chosen to do what, Mom?"

Mom: "um...well..."

Me: "Maybe they were chosen to run all the stores. Dad says the Jews own all the stores downtown like 'Broida's' and 'Friedlander's' and 'Aarons' and 'The Workingman's Store'..."

Mom: "Look, Honey, your father is a very smart man, but comparative theology is not really his strong suit." (Mom would use big words like that sometimes, just to confuse me I thought, but she did it on purpose). She said it would stretch my brain, and that's why I talk the way I do. It's not my fault. I often got headaches in my youth, and I swore it was because my Mom had stretched my brain too much and it was pushing out against the inside of my skull. I later learned that C-2 and C-3 vertebrae were misaligned due to a congenital lordosis dysfunction. See what I mean about the words? The problem was completely corrected when I was thirty-three by a miracle worker of a Chiropractor by the name of Aaron Applebaum. So God had chosen at least a few of the Jews to become Chiropractors, and I will be eternally grateful. No more headaches.

Mom continues: "No, Tommy. Listen to the nuns at catechism and don't try to learn religion from your father. As I said, it is definitely *not* his strong suit."

Me: "Which one *is* his strong suit, Mom? The blue one that he wears to church or the black one he wears when somebody croaks?"

Mom: "Don't talk like that. Not croaks—dies. When someone dies. 'Croaks' is disrespectful. People don't croak—frogs croak. People die— or better still, they pass away. But anyway, I don't mean that kind of suit. I mean the kind of suit in a deck of cards, like spades, hearts, clubs and diamonds. When someone has a strong suit it means something they are very good at. And in cards a strong suit is one you have a lot of and can do well and win your game."

And that's how I learned to play contract bridge at a very early age. I learned from the DeAngelo twins, Margaret and Anna Marie. They were very pretty. Especially Anna Marie. They looked a lot alike, but not exactly because they were not identical twins, they were "maternal" twins. They were a lot older than me, like about eleven or twelve. Older women always seemed to take a shine to me—guess that was *my* strong suit. So the three of us played bridge-Margaret and Anna Marie and me. And of course a dummy. And *I* was not the dummy.

We played after catechism class on the steps behind the church. *Saint John the Baptist Holy Roman Catholic Church,* that is.

We Can Pick a Few Greens?

About twelve miles from Clarksburg is the town of Flemington in Taylor County.

On a Sunday afternoon in the summers, we all just might pile into Zizi Thelma's Chevy and roll on down to visit the Olivio's, who were our cousins on my mother's side of the family. Sam and Ted were both barbers by trade, and they lived in the semi-country just outside of town, which was one main street and two hillsides dotted with two-story homes, well-kept and well cared for. Main street included three or four stores and a bank, a typical West Virginia small town.

Sam and Ted's mom was my mother's cousin Mary. My sister and I called her Aunt (out of respect). We called all of my mother's cousins Aunt or Uncle out of respect, but for the life of me I could never understand why "Aunt" or "Uncle" showed more respect than "Cousin," except maybe to remind them that they were older than us. Besides, I have a few cousins whom I respect as much as anyone I've ever met. But this is all very much beside the point.

Aunt Mary O. was a typical West Virginia homemaker of her time— she kept an immaculate house and was a fantastic cook. Her claim to fame, however, was her unrivaled skills at canning and preserving home-grown vegetables, fruits, and such. Mary canned tomatoes, potatoes, corn, peppers, peas, beans, beets, mushrooms, and well, just about anything that can manage to poke up out of the ground with some careful cultivating. She also "put-up" jams, jellies, preserves, sauces, pickles, relish, you name it. The walls in Mary's basement were lined with shelves from floor to ceiling with hundreds (thousands, maybe) of jars of her home-canned goods. A visit to her basement was like strolling through a gourmet supermarket.

Every jar was labeled and the shelves were stocked just like a supermarket: beans next to peas, tomato sauce next to pepper sauce, apple-butter next to apricot jam, etc. She was very particular about the appearance of her food, too. The pole beans were all standing up vertically in the jars, lined up like little green G.I.'s standing at attention.

Now home canning is not only time-consuming, but is damned hard work besides, and anyone who would take the extra effort for attractive presentation, well, it shows a lot of pride and is a good indicator of high self-esteem. (see The True Measure of a Person's Worth....)

By now you may be asking: "What does all this have to do with picking greens?" And the answer is:

"Nothing." I just thought you'd want to know that Mary Olivio was just about the best "canner" in our family, and that's saying something if you knew our family.

So one summer afternoon it has been decided by someone that my sister Barbara and I are going to accompany my Aunt Thelma and Aunt Marguerite down to Flemington to join Aunt Mary to go pick some greens, which grow wild all over the state (but you have to know just where to go exactly, and we didn't). That's where Aunt Daisy comes in—she is to be our guide and leader of the expedition. Aunt Daisy was our cousin by marriage. She was the wife of Uncle Tony. She and Tony ran a food and beverage establishment (see Beer Joints, Pinball…) in nearby Grafton, which was quite popular with the locals, and therefore, Daisy was always a storehouse of information and local gossip regarding who's expecting a new baby, who just bought a new truck, who's hiding out from the law, and where the best greens are currently growing.

So Aunt Daisy and Aunt Mary decide where we are to go green-picking, and we all pile into Zizi T's '55 Chevy 210 sedan and proceed to go (according to Daisy) "A couple of hollers down the road." Now in West Virginia, a "couple of hollers over" can be anything from a quarter of a mile to a two hour drive, depending on whether you're going with the grain (longitudinally down through the hollow) or against the grain (perpendicularly across the hollow).

After bouncing around on a one-lane road for a short time, we arrive at our destination- a "used to be farm" with a nondescript one story frame house commanding the entrance to a small hill, on the other side of which is a huge green meadow.
A sleepy-looking lady comes out on the front porch wondering why this car full of strangers have invaded her solitude, and our spokesperson and front man (Aunt Daisy) calls out in her beautiful Italian accent:

"Hello, hello! 'Sorright we pick a few greens?"

Undoubtedly wondering why anyone would want to go traipsing over a meadow picking greens on a day that has reached about ninety-five degrees, when one could easily open up a cold beer and watch "Days of our Lives" The lady says,

"Shore, but don' go pickin' over by at-air tree- tha dawg's bin sick over there."

Yeah, I know. I look at my sister and I'm not sure if she's going to throw-up or die laughing.

So the lady adds, "Up over at-air rise is the best place right over yonder." Now a word or two for those who may not be familiar with the term "yonder" and its derivatives, as used in the hollows of the mountain states:

Up yonder: away from here, and somewhat higher in elevation, as in;

"We had to go up yonder, 'cause the crick was fixin' to rise"

Down yonder: lower in elevation than where you currently are, as in:
"They got a helluva fiddle player down yonder at Lefty's joint."

Out yonder: Away from the town, the house, anywhere that is somewhat removed from the center of attention, as in:

"We got a shed out yonder where we keep the hay rake."

Back yonder: deeper into the woods or back from where from you just came, as in:

"Ya gotta go back yonder about a mile, and turn down the dirt road."

Over yonder; you're going to have to go up and down at least one hill to get there, as in;

"Mary's place is over yonder about a half mile."
And of course, there's just plain…

Yonder; could be just about any direction, any distance, but usually connotes something visible to the naked eye, as in;

"Yonder comes Billy with a big sack. Waddaya ' spose he's lookin' to borry now?"

So the six of us set out "over yonder," armed to the teeth with big sharp hickory-handled kitchen knives, aprons, and paper bags (plastic trash bags not having been invented yet, or at least not readily available). Cresting the small rise we see a beautiful meadow; there is one solitary cow quietly grazing, paying us no mind, and one baleful-looking hound dog circling us at a safe distance, pausing occasionally to look at up and bark (protecting his meadow, no doubt, from these odd knife-and-bag-bearing strangers, who are possibly seeking to irrevocably alter his placid way of life).

Part of the lush green of the aforementioned meadow was indeed a splendid crop of dandelions and a few wild turnips and mustards, but the dandelions were what we were stalking this particular day.

Since I was just a boy, and could not be relied upon to distinguish a dandelion from an azalea bush, I was therefore not trusted with a knife, but my job was to carry the bags for the ladies, and run from one to the other, who would call to me when her apron was full and ready to be transferred into a bag.

So, relegated to do the extremely important role of pack-mule, I scurried from one Aunt to the another, and was therefore the first one to notice that we had picked enough greens to feed the Pittsburgh Pirates and their families, but that apparently did not matter. When these women saw this field of greens ("field of dreams" to a green-picker), they got a glazed look in their eyes and fanned-out over the perimeter, avoided both the cow and dog, and systemically invaded the meadow much like Stonewall Jackson outflanked General Irvin's troops at the first battle of Bull Run (Manassas Junction #I).

I believed we would have picked that field clean of all plant life, had not a dark storm cloud appeared (I think it was "over yonder"), and even the cow had enough sense to start heading to the barn.

Back down the hill, arriving at the Chevy, we pile the bags into the trunk and it is filled completely to the brim and then some, and looking at the take, Aunt Daisy is remembered to comment,

"Gee, we did pretty good, huh?"

So back down the road to Flemington everybody is trying to think of who would like a big bag of greens, Aunt Daisy says, "Tony Veltri, will take one", and Zizi T. says,

"Frances will take one and our sister Rosie"- my mother, the "Greens Queen" of Clarksburg. She loved them, and my dad did too. Mom made them all and was well acquainted with all varieties— dandelions, turnip greens, mustard greens, chicory, collards, watercress, romaine, escarole, endive (straight and curly), spinach, red leaf, Boston, curly bib, and radicchio. Yes, we had them all. But to me they were all the same— a salad is a salad. I was not a big fan of salad.

But still I feel that our lives were somehow enriched by eating such a variety of greens. While the poor unknowing folk of Central West Virginia who were not fortunate enough to be either a hillbilly or an Italian struggled along with only iceberg lettuce, we had salad with color, texture, and taste varying from mild to strong, sweet to bitter, pungently aromatic to somewhat nutty in flavor. We had options. We had variety. We had choices.

We can pick a few greens.

Spinach Minestra with Hamhocks.

Ingredients:
4 smoked ham-hocks *
1 Medium Onion
2 cloves of garlic
1 large bag fresh or 2 pkgs. frozen chopped spinach (whole leaf, sliced into quarters) **
5 medium baking potatoes
1 cup of water
Butter or olive oil
½ teaspoon Crushed red pepper
Substitutions:
(*) Possible substitutions for Ham-hock: ½ pound of sliced bacon.
(**)Possible substitutions for spinach: Turnip greens
                                        Mustard greens
                                        Mixed greens
                                        Dandelions
                                        Green beans
Directions:
Cut bacon into 1' pieces and cook until crisp, drain grease (save for onions), crumble and set to the side. Peel and slice potatoes 1/8 inch thin. Peel and finely chop garlic. Sauté onion in bacon grease until transluscent. Cook spinach fresh 15 minutes, frozen (follow package directions). Add a couple ounces of water to a Dutch oven. Put in potatoes, onions, spinach, olive oil, and red pepper. Bring to a boil, reduce heat and simmer for 45 minutes. Add bacon back in, simmer additional 45 minutes.
Serve with a sprinkle of parmesan and garlic bread.

The Bus Trip to Pittsburgh

It was in the summer—almost every summer. My dad was busy working—the height of the season at the country club. My sister and I were on vacation from school. My mother would take Barb and I to Pittsburgh for a few days to visit Uncle John and Aunt Teresa. Sometimes one or two of my Aunts would join us in what seemed to be part vacation and past pilgrimage.

For me, going to Pittsburgh was like what going to Mecca must have been to Muslims. Or like going in to Omaha for a couple of Nebraska farm kids. Later on in life I learned that some of the kids from rural West Virginia got a big charge out of going into Clarksburg on occasion. But growing up in Clarksburg, to me it was always small potatoes.

Pittsburgh, on the other hand was the real deal. This was the big city. This was a place that was known all over the world. The Pirates. The Steelers. H.J. Heinz. Andrew Carnegie. The steelmills. "In a Pawn Shop on a Corner in Pittsburgh, Pennsylvania." The Big Time.

The trip was never exactly the same, but there were mandatory features that always seemed to stand out in a child's mind. It wouldn't be a trip to Pittsburgh without these essential elements. The trolley cars. The traffic. The street vendors. The black smoke spewing out of the big stacks at the mills. The white and yellow smoke drifting up from the breweries. The barges on the river. The Allegheny, the Ohio and, the Monongahela.

The trip started out at the bus station in Clarksburg—The Interurban Terminal, a kind of warehouse-looking place with buses from all over belching out diesel fumes like gas from a volcano. I loved the smell. The signs in front of the buses told their destination. Exotic places like Erie, Cleveland, Washington, D.C. And then finally the one we were waiting for—Pittsburgh. All right—here we go. If we were lucky it would be a Greyhound Scenic Cruiser with the back two-thirds of the passenger coach raised up a couple of feet for a better view. A bathroom right on the bus. Not a lavatory or toilet or restroom—in West Virginia everything was called a bathroom. I remember thinking, "Wow! Scenic Cruiser with a bathroom – this is really first class!"

Finally the terminal conductor would call for everyone bound for Pittsburgh to board. The best seats were the first row on the top level: not only did you get the scenic view of everything outside, but you could watch the bus driver as he expertly maneuvered this behemoth in heavy city traffic and on the curvy mountain roads of West Virginia. This was pre-interstate, and riding on the top level of a Greyhound in the mountains was closely akin to riding at half-speed on the "Jack Rabbit" roller coaster at Kennywood Park.

The trip was about three or four hours, but seemed much longer than that. The towns came and went with quick stops to pick up and drop off passengers—Fairmont, Morgantown, Uniontown, and Monessen.

Finally the whole world went black as the Greyhound

entered the Fort Pitt Tunnel. Entering Pittsburgh from the south was especially dramatic, because as you exited the tunnel you were greeted by an unbelievable vista—the confluence of the three rivers. The Golden Triangle. Downtown Pittsburgh. Mount Washington on the left—the incline. At this point someone had to start singing "Finiculi, Finicula." It's a ritual.

Crossing the Mon into the city, we passed the US Steel Building, the old hotels like the Fort Pitt, Penn Station, and finally pulled into the bus terminal.   Boy, if you thought the one in Clarksburg was big, this one was huge—and the names on the buses showed that people went from Pittsburgh to darn near anywhere: Philadelphia, Buffalo, Syracuse, Boston, Chicago, Detroit, and New York.

Uncle John was always there to meet us at the station. The ride in Uncle John's big car (a Chrysler if memory serves) back to their home in Aspinwall took us across the Allegheny where you could see downtown from another angle. Past the Iron City Brewery and the H.J. Heinz Factory, a compound of large old red brick buildings which seemed to go on forever along the river. It looked like a place where they made freight trains, not ketchup and pickles.

Uncle John and Aunt Teresa lived in a large, three story yellow brick house which seemed like a throwback to another time. Elms, oaks, and maples lined both sides of the street in this older residential section of Aspinwall, and there was a service road in the back where the garages were. They had a large back yard with a rose garden, and a big vegetable garden. Even in the city old Italians always had a garden and Uncle John was no exception. He enjoyed growing tomatoes, peppers, green beans, cucumbers, onions, etc.

By the time I was old enough to go to Pittsburgh, Uncle John was retired from the steel mills where he worked his entire adult life, so he had nothing but time on his hands and seemed to enjoy entertaining guests by carting us around to wherever we wanted to go, and he seemed to particularly enjoy taking me with him whenever he went out. A big, burly gruff-talking man with a heavy Italian accent, which living forty years in Pittsburgh couldn't put a dent into, his rough exterior mannerisms could not conceal the gentle, loving soul that he was. Both he and Aunt Teresa were always genuinely excited to see their relatives from West Virginia.

The big old house in Aspinwall was furnished with heavy wooden furniture from the thirties, forties, and fifties. The large stairways in the front and rear of the house led to the second floor hallway which ran the entire length of the house. This gave me the opportunity to run up the front stairs, tear down the hallway, and emerge back downstairs in the kitchen. How cool is that?

A lot of family pictures hung on the walls. Oriental rugs on the hardwood floors. The whole house was a little on the dark side, the windows heavily draped. Except for Aunt Teresa's kitchen, which was huge and very well lit from several large windows. Like most Italian families, this was where we would spend hour after hour eating, drinking coffee, and catching up on what was going on in this or that cousin's life—who was going to college, who was working where, who got married, who had a new baby, etc.

Suddenly Aunt Teresa would get a brainstorm about something which needed to be gotten at this or that store immediately, or who was in dire need of an impromptu visit from the West Virginia bunch, and she would call out to Uncle John in her contralto booming voice,

"Gian,wa pia la machina !", which meant, "Quick, John, go get the car!" It wasn't a car or even an automobile, it was to her "the machine." So Uncle John, the interminable sufferer of all Aunt Teresa's demands, would mutter something under his breath, grab his hat and a cigar which he never lit, and go trudging out the back door to the garage only to appear a few minutes later in the front of the house parked at the curb, honking the horn. Aunt Teresa always had to leave from the front of the house, as good breeding would dictate, especially with four or five out-of- town relatives in tow.

It didn't matter if we were going to visit the Intriri's in Sharpsburg—Teresa, Mary, Amadeo, Louie and Willie, or just a quick run to the Italian market for a couple pounds of cappacola, we all had to go, and we had to go right now! Poor Uncle John.

Every now and then Uncle John would whisper to me,

"Hey Tommy – want to go for a ride?" And we would sneak out the back, pretending to go pick a tomato, and he would have the car running and we would sneak off and go driving around to no place in particular—I think this was his way of getting a short vacation from the rattle of all the hens coming from the kitchen.

I loved riding around in Pittsburgh—I knew about Pittsburgh because in Northern West Virginia all our TV stations originated in Pittsburgh. Oh, sure, we had a local TV station in Clarksburg, but it was definitely third rate. It had the small-town sound, look and feel to it that comes from poor studio facilities, and local never-will-make-it-big TV personalities. The staff consisted of about four people. The news anchorman was also the sportscaster, weatherman, and did most of the voice-overs. A wig and mustache and funny hat and presto—Peter Lyman became "Uncle Pete" the host of the after-school kiddie show. This, of course fooled no-one, not even us kids, who saw Mr. Lyman driving past our house to the television studio about four times every day.

But Pittsburgh was different. I knew something about Pittsburgh before I ever went there. The TV Shows— Studio Wrestling, Bowling for Dollars with Nick Perry. A special hello to the folks in Corriopolis, or Squirrel Hill, or McKees Rocks, or McKeesport, Oakland, or Alliquippa. I loved the sound of that place—*Alliquippa!* Probably a Native American word meaning: "Place where two rivers join and the air is gray and they make steel and beer and pickles"—Alliquippa!

The Friday night scary movie with Chilly Billy Cardilli. The Steelers. The Pirate games with Bob Prince on the radio. Vernon Law on the mound . Elroy Face in the bullpen. Dick Stuart on first, Bill Verdon in center, Dick Groat at short, and Bill Mazeroski at second—the Golden

Glove, the "Hoover". Two years later Maz would knock one over Yogi Berra's head in the seventh game of the world series.

Yes, Forbes Field was always my favorite spot to visit in Pittsburgh. And later there was Willie Stargell and Manny Mota and Matty Alou and Clemente. My dad and I got tickets in the right field bleachers just to watch "The Great One" throw somebody out at the plate.

A trip to Pittsburgh wasn't complete without a day at the Zoo. Not a petting zoo that travels around the country, oh no! The Pittsburgh Zoo was one of the best in the world in it's day. Lions, tigers, giraffes, rhinos, hippos, you name it. My favorites were the elephants— just don't see a lot of elephants in West Virginia.

Of course, with me being the only male in the troop of tourist hillbillies, I had to suffer several shopping trips downtown, but even that was bearable because the big department stores were something we just didn't have back home. Gimbel's, Kaufman's, Macy's. There's something lost in big sprawling shopping malls. Give me the big city downtown department store any day. From a bygone era, these stores were like towns unto themselves. You could have breakfast, shop, get a haircut, watch TV, have lunch, shop some more, get your shoes re-soled, get fitted for a suit, have dinner, and never leave the store.

To a seven year old, the best thing about these stores was the escalators—we had no escalators in Clarksburg. The idea of riding on a moving stairway just captivated me. It doesn't take much to impress a hillbilly—you couldn't get me off the darned thing:

"Hey look Mom, there's ladies' accessories on the seventh floor—don't you need some of those? Let's go up there !"

"You don't fool me—you just want to ride the escalator!" And I'm thinking,

"No kidding." As a kid I wanted to ride anything—an elevator, a pony, a merry-go-round, a see-saw, a roller coaster, bumper cars, an old truck, a bicycle, a hay wagon. If it moves, then yes, I want to ride it. Why not an escalator? Interesting thing about the escalators in Gimbel's. They get narrower as you go up to the higher floors. It makes sense—less traffic on the upper floors. And on the very top two floors, the metal grates gave way to very rickety old wooden grates which were just wide enough for a person to stand and they make a click-clack sound which made you think they were going to fall apart just any second. I loved these last two, of course, and it always took some convincing for me to get Mom to check out the eleventh and twelfth floors, because the only thing they sold up there was like office equipment or something.

Across the street from Gimbel's was the first Indian Restaurant I ever saw, and I wanted to have lunch there, but the ladies explained that it wasn't the kind of Indians I was expecting and I probably wouldn't like the food, which meant *they* probably wouldn't like the food, and Tonto most assuredly would not be at the Indian Restaurant.

So I settled for a trolley-car ride down to the Brass Rail,

which was a really good place to have lunch. After that, a quick trip to the Carnegie Museum to stuff some culture into my seven-year-old brain.

Another trolley ride and three stuffed dinosaurs later, Barb is telling Mom there's a Gaugin in the next room, and I correct her, "It's not a Gaugin—it's a Rodan," and she says,

"Not the dinosaur, silly. I'm talking about the painting. And these in this room are all Botticelli." So I'm guessing "Botticelli" is the Italian word for big ol' fat ladies, 'cause that's what they were, and why are we wasting time looking at pictures of big ol' fat ladies when there are plenty of them back home in Clarksburg. Of course, to a seven year old, anyone over thirty is old and anyone over a hundred and twenty is fat. Why, even in my own family you can't hardly swing a cat around by the tail without hitting a big ol' fat lady. Looking at all the culture, I'm wondering if Bob Friend is on the mound tonight—sure would be nice to catch a game this trip. I bet Uncle John would like to sneak out for a couple hours away from the hens and maybe actually light up that cigar of his.

But Friend wasn't pitching that night. Kline was starting and Uncle John didn't like Kline, and he said he didn't want to go to a night game, 'cause he falls asleep in about the fourth inning, so,

"Lets go tomorrow, Tommy—it's a double header (Friend and Law)". Baseball is better in the daytime anyway—any Cubs' fan will tell ya that.

Are that was fine by me—got to see Groat and Maz turn a double play, and Stuart hit one out in the second inning, and the Pirates beat the Phillies both games. We had pop and hot dogs and Uncle John took me over to the bullpen where you can stand behind a cyclone fence right behind the catcher (Smoky Burgess, I think) while he warmed up the relievers. I think that was the day I decided not to become a professional baseball player. Maybe basketball— I never saw anyone throw a basketball so fast you couldn't see it.

That night Aunt Teresa made Pasta Fagioli and roasted peppers with steak. Our vacation over, the next day Uncle John drove us to the bus station and its back to West Virginia.

All things considered, a very exciting week. I got to see skyscrapers, dinosaurs, three home runs, a Gaugin, Elroy Face striking out the side to end game one, elephants, at least three Botticelli's, rode the Thunderbolt at Kennywood, and did not have lunch at an Indian restaurant.

Coming back to Clarksburg, I'm feeling very cosmopolitan and worldly, and the next time Nick Perry welcomes the crowd from McKeesport I can say "I been there!"

Mushroom Hunting

As earlier mentioned, part of the dichotomy of growing up as an Italian Hillbilly, is due to the fact that sometimes the cultures of Italian immigrants and American pioneers may overlap, and the child just learning the ways of the world may not always know to which of the two worlds those ways belong.

Take Mushrooms, for example. "Mushrooms?", you say? Well, yes. Italians, like most Europeans, like to eat mushrooms, and fix them in a variety of ways. And American pioneers relied heavily on the bounty provided to them by the forests, and Appalachia was no exception. The folks who settled in West Virginia during the eighteenth and nineteenth centuries had often been rural folk back in the old country (didn't matter *which* old country), and even if they were not, they quickly became dependent on and knowledgeable of the American forest. The American woodsmen (and women) relied on the forest for not only fuel, building materials and game to hunt, but also for its plentiful supply of nuts, berries, and other treasures. Among these other treasures was the wild mushroom.

Mycophagy (the art of consuming mushrooms) dates to ancient times (several hundred years B.C. in China, for example). Mushrooms were prized by the ancient Greeks and Romans, particularly the upper and ruling classes of society.

To those who would go searching in the wild for edible mushrooms—a word of caution: The Roman Caesars always had a food taster who would eat the mushrooms first to ensure their safe consumption. If you yourself do not have a professional food taster employed in your household, never, *but never,* eat a wild mushroom unless you are absolutely sure that it is one of the edible variety. Poisonous mushrooms often bear a striking resemblance to their edible counterparts.

Several members of my own family, being both Italians and West Virginians, really knew their mushrooms. My own father was considered to be quite an authority, and would often go out traipsing through the woods to gather these little goodies. Morels in the springtime, other varieties throughout the summer, and in the autumn, my favorite, the *Grifola Polypilus Frondosa,* or as it is sometimes referred to in the Mountain State, the *Hen of the Woods.* It derives this nickname from its resemblance to a Rooster's Comb. In Italian it is called the *Pettine de Gallo*; my Grandmother called it *Cherche Gallo.* I make mention of this particular variety, because , in my opinion it is the tastiest of all the wild mushrooms. All the current rage about Shitake's and Portobella's, why, they pale in comparison to the Hen of the Woods! And the regular variety of white button mushrooms—these are to Cherche Gallo's what instant vanilla pudding is to Crème Brule'! They must have been my dad's favorite as well, for he would always seem to know where to find the biggest and best ones, and would spare no effort to bring home this prize, often and in great quantity.

Mushrooms seemed to play a bigger part in my young life than perhaps should have been the case. For example, there was the time when my kindergarten teacher, Mrs. Pinnell, called my mother to ask her what a "Voongee" was. Apparently we were learning new words, and were told to identify simple pictures of things, one of which was a mushroom. I wrote (yes, I could *write* in kindergarten, thanks to Mom) "Voongee" next to the picture of the toadstool or whatever. My mother informed the teacher that I was using the Italian word "Fungi", but apparently could not spell it. This is a prime example of a little kid suffering from culture clash.

And so it was that I often found myself running around in the woods with my father picking blackberries in the summer, hickory nuts or black walnuts in the fall, and mushrooms damn near anytime. I used to think that my dad was the world's foremost authority on wild mushrooms, or at least in the top ten, because he always seemed to know which ones were which, and would go on and on about this kind or that, and how good they are, and how to pick them.

"Now see, Tommy, you've got to surround the bottom of the stalk with your fingers, and lift the whole thing out, don't just snap it off at the stem." "And see this one here?" "Don't ever pick one of these, they're poison!"
Whenever we came across a bad one, Dad would stomp on it and grind it into the earth so that it wouldn't make spores and populate the forest. It was his way of showing disdain for the evil fungi and at the same time protecting other hunters from confusing a harmless little Morel from the deadly Galerina.

We always had with us the mandatory mushroom man's supply kit. A bushel basket for carrying the mushrooms, a brush to clean them (a paint brush, usually, in our case), and a sharp knife. My father worked as the manager at the country club, which in this case, was actually *in* the country, and the four-mile drive back into town (where we lived) was by way of a two-lane road which meandered through the woods. Deep woods. Dark woods. Hansel and Gretel-type woods. Mushroom-filled woods.

It was on just such a return from work (I had been at the club that day, swimming and hanging out) that Dad suddenly got a premonition or something, and decided that there were mushrooms for the taking. Coming to a dead stop, he slammed the '56 Star Chief into reverse and parked by the side of the road next to a particularly wooded area.

"Hey, Tommy! I betcha there's some good mushrooms down by those fallen trees!" Not trusting me with the knife, and for good reason, here I am following Dad, lugging the peach basket which was about as big as I was, and trying to keep up with him, which is no mean feat, 'cause my dad could walk through dense woods about as fast as a Black Bear. We went over about two or three hills, which were probably only very small knolls in reality, but to a six-year-old seemed like Mount Whitney- and suddenly Dad stops in his tracks and gives out a low whistle. The low whistle was my Dad's way of saying "Holy Shit!", but he never swore. Not around us kids, at least. There in front of us, on a hollowed-out old log, was the biggest mushroom I had ever seen. It was growing in ridges along almost the entire length of this very large fallen tree trunk. This was no doubt the find of the century—my dad is the best person to have along on a mushroom hunt you could find. He's got the instincts of a truffle pig. I'm thinking we're gonna just hack away at this mother and bring it back to the car, but Dad has another idea.

"It's not ready yet—we'll come back later."

So every evening for about a week we stop by the same woods to check on it, never parking in the same place in case someone is watching us and finds out our secret and beats us to this "king of all mushrooms". We even approached from a different direction each time in case we were under surveillance.

Surveillance by whom I wondered? The mushroom police? The FBI (Fungus Bureau of Intelligence)?

"Hey Dad—want I should pitch a tent and just hang here for a few days to make sure nobody beats us to it?" I remember thinking that mushrooms must have some sort of time bomb in them which would go off when ready, and give a signal known only by the local Indian medicine men of the long-gone Seneca era (and of course, my dad).

Finally, one evening we stop by the side of the road as usual, and when we get to the hollow log, Dad exclaims:

"It's ready."

I remember thinking that maybe we should chant and do a dance around it, light a fire, or make some sort of sacrificial offering to the *Voongee* God, or at least say a prayer to the patron Saint of Fungal Species, like maybe *Saint Lichen of Nice,* for example. And speaking of which, did you ever wonder just how much jurisdiction a patron saint of lower plant forms would have? For example, would he be limited to fungus, or would he be allowed to hear and process prayers covering a broader spectrum? Like from one-celled Euglenae up through and including say, the mosses, or even ferns, perhaps? I always like to think that some leeway is given on the receiving end of such prayers, because what if you prayed to the wrong saint? This sometimes worried me as a child. If you got a hold of the wrong saint, would they not know what you were talking about, or would they just not listen? Or do they have some sort of forwarding system where they could route the prayer to the correct department? I think they must have, because otherwise you would have people's prayers being ignored, since we all have different interpretations on things. For example, all us little Catholic kids knew that if you lose something you pray to Saint Anthony—Patron Saint of the Lost. And if you are traveling you pray to Saint Christopher—Patron Saint of Travelers. But what if you lose a traveler? Or your car? See the problem? Or worse—let's say you're out fishing on the bay one day, and a big storm comes up? Naturally you would offer up a prayer to Saint Peter, the protector of fishermen; but what if it's a thunder storm? Should you then pray to Santa Barbara (crossing yourself, of course)? Or is it okay to incorporate the two together, as in: "Dear Barb and Pete, get this sinner to the shore!"

This, I think, is a great philosophical conundrum. But not to a mushroom. Mushrooms do not think that deeply. For one thing, they do not live all that long. And I believe they also suffer from low self esteem. You would too if you were always kept in the dark and people were always trying to feed you a bunch of crap. No, mushrooms lead a very simple existence. But they can be clever, however. Dad would see them from far off, but my first clue was usually the squishing sound coming from under my foot, as I would slowly creep through the woods, trying to simulate Hiawatha. Or Daniel Boone stalking the elusive *Morchella Conica.*

But they're crafty, these mushrooms. They tend to surround themselves with rotting leaves and twigs and such, and can be quite invisible to a six-year-old city boy. Not that Clarksburg could be thought of as the big city, exactly, but does not have mushrooms growing in the streets (or at least it didn't in 1957). Twilight—when every sharp twig in the forest goes right for your eyes, when you stub your toe on every rock and bang your skinny shins into every fallen tree. Looking for the little white caps among the leaves on the forest floor, or the bronze shimmer of the layered ones on old logs. The tall, thin, tan ones that grow in the short grass by the tree line. Pick them up, cut and carry. Back to the car, a good night's hunt. The cubs will eat well tonight. Oh, but not tonight—no, no, the fun's just begun.

They must be cleaned and washed immediately when you get home. I remember Mom or Nana standing at the kitchen sink, turning each mushroom over and gently washing each little gill on the underside, making sure there are no bugs, or dirt, or worms. Tiny little worms like mushrooms too, and Mom would let out a blood curdling scream if she found one, run into the other room, wring her hands for a second or too, and go right back to the sink.. She did not like little crawly things. But she went right back to washing them anyway. Such is the toughness of the Italian, West Virginian, American Pioneer housewife who would wish her family to have these wonderful, tasty morsels. Picking a handful or two and sautéing them with onions to put on tonight's steak is one thing, but we ate them a hundred different ways, and all year long—in and out of season.

Cooking up a few is easy. But what do you do when confronted with the monster that Dad and I brought home that night when the big *Pettine de Gallo* from Hell was finally "ready"? This bastard entirely filled up the trunk of the Pontiac! I'm not exaggerating one bit. We stopped off at Nana's house to give her a bushel or so, and brought the rest home. And what was done with a trunk-full of mushroom? It was canned—put up in jars for later.

Washing, cleaning, cutting, boiling water for the jars. Canned in water, canned in tomato sauce with ripe bell peppers or onions, or by themselves. My favorite is with red bell peppers in tomato sauce with garlic and basil. Dried, cooled, labeled, and set up on a shelf in the basement. Opened several months later, when you have forgotten how much work they were to do.

As a young child I could never understand why anyone would go to all that time and effort to collect and prepare something that is, biologically speaking, only one step away from mold. You know why? I'll tell ya why— because it is a delicacy! That is how Dad explained it to me. It was a *DELICACY!* That was the word he used to describe anything that was notoriously awful smelling, tasting, or looking. And he would say the word with such relish—*Delicacy!*

"So what's this we're having tonight, Dad? Looks like rat's ass to me".

"Why, Tommy, in Singapore rat's ass is a real *Delicacy!* People will drive a long way and pay a lot of money to get their hands on some of this! Come on, try some. You don't know what you're missing!"

"I'll take that chance, Dad."

And then there was the time (also back at the country club) when Uncle Mario found that nice stand (that's what they're called—a *stand,* like a yoke of oxen, a murder of crows, a stand of mushrooms) down behind the seventeenth green. I helped him pick them and we put them in the trunk of Dad's car.

"Don't tell your dad." Uncle Mario said. "Surprise him when you get home."

And was he ever surprised! We pulled into Fairview Avenue, found a good parking spot right near the corner, got out, and I'm squealing,

"Dad! Open the Trunk!"

"Open the trunk? Why? What For? Okay, okay, well—who put these in here?" To which I reply:

"I cannot tell a lie". (I said that a lot, having learned about Washington; but the reality was, I *could* most certainly tell a lie, and did quite often, though I'm not sure why. I just think it made life more interesting). "Out of respect to you, oh great Mushroom Hunter, the Starchief has taken to growing her own—in the trunk. No, really— *I* found them. No, really—an old witch…"

"I'll bet your Uncle Mario found these." There was no fooling Dad. Those old mushroom guys must have a secret society among themselves. Probably have their own secret handshake and decoder rings, too.

Another one was my Uncle Johnny—now he could fix up a mess of Voongee, too. As I mentioned earlier, I was partial to my mother's *fungi e pepe*, but there were others, like plain in water, for further processing, olive oil and garlic, and even *fungi e tripe* (don't even ask). Speaking of my Uncle John, there was the time when my Cousin John Barberio and I were fooling around over at the meadow across the ravine by their house, when we spotted what appeared to be really nice mushrooms and decided to impress both his dad and mine by picking them and bringing them home, rather than waste our time just goofing off. But when we got back to the house, Zizi John and my dad had a real good laugh, since what we picked were just "puffballs" and apparently worthless. So instead of tossing a ball around, or doing something fun, we were held up to ridicule for trying to do something useful. As I said, If you don't know what you're doing, stay out of the woods and buy your mushrooms at the supermarket. They won't taste as good, but you'll not die a painful and embarrassing death, either.

Yes, the old mushroom guys like my dad and Zizi Johnny (Charter members, no doubt) really knew their 'shrooms. I could envision them sitting around a kitchen table with a loaf of fresh bread, maybe a wedge of strong cheese, and a jar of "fixed" olives. (A "fixed olive" is one who will never have little olives, apparently). Suddenly, one of these great connoisseurs of wild mushrooms will reach over and grab a jar of the little devils, open it up, take a good sniff of the contents, and proclaim loudly:

"Davison Run-'57! Now *that* was *some* mushroom! Liked to wore me out; found him sticking out from under the log. Two trips to get him into the car. Put up a hell of a fight. But isn't it gooood now? MmmmMmmm!"

I thought all kids went mushroom hunting with their fathers. Found out at school later that all the kids who did, including me, was exactly *one.* Once again, the cultural adjustment. I started to think that maybe stalking wild mushrooms was not the coolest thing to do in 1957. So I never discussed it with my pals at school. Until one day I fessed up—I had gone out to look for them with my dad on a Saturday instead of playing football. All the guys laughed and said things like,

"Why the hell would you do that, for God's sake?"

"Because they're a *Delicacy,* Godammit! And if you weren't such a stupid snuffy you would know it!"

Fact of the matter is, now with all the fancy restaurants serving *Shitake* this, and *Portobella* that, none of which can even hold a candle to my family's *fungi*, fresh or canned, turned out my dad was right.

And I tell you the truth—every time I order an antipasto of Portobella mushrooms or similar fare, I can't help but regret how truly inferior they are to my Mom's *Chercha Gallo e Pepe.* Fact is, I'd drive a long way and pay a lot of money.....

Making Ravioli with Nana

Of all the great Italian dishes I ate growing up, my all-time favorite was my grandmother's homemade ravioli. We didn't have it all that often, maybe two or three times a year. The main reason for this was probably because it is a lot of work (not that that ever stopped anyone), and takes a long time to prepare from scratch. Making a Sunday dinner of homemade ravioli for fifteen to twenty aunts, uncles and cousins usually meant we would be making it on a Saturday and it would take most of a full day.

If you're going to make a batch to serve four people however, divide my recipe by one-fourth and count on about 2 hours of preparation time.

Making ravioli at Nana's house was a big production. The kitchen, the basement kitchen, and the dining room were turned into a pasta factory for the performance. Directed by my Nana, the supporting cast usually consisted of a couple aunts, my mother, my sister and myself.

This production very much resembled a play in five acts:
      Act 1: the dough
      Act 2: the filling
      Act 3: the assembly
      Act 4: the sauce
      Act 5: the cooking of the pasta

Act 1

The scene opens with Nana in the basement kitchen. She

has cleared the big table in the middle of the room and washed down the surface. She has placed her dough pan, a large tin basin about 20 inches in diameter and 5 or 6 inches deep, in the center of the table, into which she puts about 20 cups of unbleached white flour. Robin Hood brand flour—her favorite and nothing less would do. She is clad in a flowered print house dress and a large white apron. Her hair is pulled back into a bun with a white scarf covering her head. She is now ready for combat. She begins by making a large hole in the middle of the flour with her hands, looking not unlike Moses parting the Red Sea. Into the hole she drops about 8 or 10 eggs. She breaks and beats the eggs slightly with a fork. Pulling the flour into the center, she mixes the mixture thoroughly adding a little warm water now and then to get the right stiff consistency. How much and when to add the water was always a mystery to me. I think it is an instinctual thing—probably genetic in origin. It's a feeling, not a thought process. Much like a PGA Tour golfer standing over a thirty foot put which goes downhill against the grain breaking left to right with a slight helping breeze. You just have to feel it. She then kneads the dough by pushing, pulling, punching, turning, and rolling it for quite a long while. She is singing Italian songs during this whole process. I believe it is mandatory to sing Italian songs while kneading the dough. If you personally do not know an Italian song, just put on a Dean Martin album or CD and hum along. "When the moon hits the sky like a big pizza pie, that's amore!" *

Halfway thru " 'Twas on the Isle of Capri" the dough will be finished. When the dough is smooth enough for Nana's satisfaction, she covers it with a linen cloth and lets it rest for 15 minutes. The dough must rest, but not Nana. Being the director, she must trundle up the basement steps to check on the rest of the cast, who are in the upstairs kitchen making the ravioli filling.

Walking around the kitchen from station to station, she peers over everyone's shoulder nodding her satisfaction. After she has inspected everyone's work, she pauses to turn and face the cast members and proclaims,

" Buono, Buono, tiene a andare." ("Good, Good, Keep going.") She will now return to the basement to finish the dough. She does this alone because no one but Nana is allowed to make the dough. It's permissible to watch her, but she is bound and determined to do all the heavy lifting. There are two reasons for this:

#1: She's the Nana, which to an Italian family is like the "Goddess of the Hearth" , and you don't mess with her, and,

#2: If Da Vinci offers to paint your garage, you do not offer to help him. Okay, maybe hand him a brush now and then, but that's about all.

This is about the time I set aside my parsley chopping or whatever, and follow Nana down the basement steps. I am not about to miss the next scene, the tour de force of the performance, the rolling of the dough.

Removing the linen cloth, Nana examines the dough, smiles and announces to no one in particular,

" Penso che e pronto." ("I think it's ready.") Putting the big pan of dough on the counter, she lightly flours the tabletop. After cutting off a portion of the dough (about 1/8 of it in my estimation,(half of it if you are using the recipe for 4 servings), she places the dough on the table surface and reaches overhead for her rolling pin which is hanging by a string from a nail in the basement ceiling. Now when I say "rolling pin" you must understand that this is not your standard rolling pin found in most kitchens. Nana has one of those, of course, in fact she has several for making a pie-crust or whatever, but for this job she reaches for the Big Kahuna. The dough-rolling pin is actually a pole about four feet long and about an inch and a half in diameter.

After flouring the surface of the rolling pin, she places herself squarely in front of the table, bent over slightly at the waist, her feet about 5 inches apart, weight resting on the balls of her feet. Dressed almost entirely in white, rolling pin at chest height, she is now ready for combat. I'm sitting on a tall stool wide-eyed with anticipation, for my mild-mannered Italian grandmother is about to become "Ninja Nana!" She begins by rolling the dough on the surface of the table, but with the adroitness of a master of the martial arts, she is soon lifting the flattened dough off the surface of the table and flipping it up into the air where it turns over as commanded, exactly one half turn and she catches it on the other side with the pin and flips it up again. The only thing missing are the Kung-Fu sound effects such as "Heeyaaaii!"

I am more than happy to supply the sound effects for her and from the corner, stage right, I am reciting my self-assigned lines of,

"Whoooooooo and Haaaaa !" Nana, however is not a big fan of ad-libbing apparently, and hits me with a sidelong glance which, without any words says,

"Let's show a little respect, Tommy, this is, after all, the Body of Christ."

Nana continues with the rolling and flipping and singing until she has about eight sheets which are about 1/16 to 1/8 inch thick.

"When the stars start to shine like you've had too much wine, that's amore!" *

Meanwhile, up in the main kitchen, the supporting cast with Thelma as co-star is preparing the filling. There are literally dozens of fillings for ravioli, probably the most common of which is the basic cheese variety. For your four-serving recipe, this would be:

1½ lbs ricotta cheese, drained
¼ lb (about 1 cup) freshly grated Romano cheese
2 eggs, slightly beaten
salt & pepper to taste.

Other popular fillings include:

Italian Sausage
Mushroom
Shellfish (lobster, crab or shrimp) an Alfredo Sauce would be very appropriate here.

But for the day-long preparation, Sunday dinner for 15 or so hungry Italians, we are doing the meat and spinach filling which is the favorite of most everyone in our family, most everyone being me and several others. The several others include Zizi Johnny B (maybe) and Dyane (maybe) and Tommy Diaz (maybe) . . . well, me anyway.

The meat and spinach filling recipe for the whole clan includes:

5 lbs lean ground beef (could use ½ beef and ½ veal)
4 tbls. butter
4 cloves garlic
3 cups cooked chopped spinach, squeezed dry
4 tbls. parsley, chopped
8 eggs, slightly beaten
10 tbls. freshly grated Romano cheese

ACT II
The Filling

The scene opens in the upstairs kitchen. Zizi Thelma is browning the beef in butter with the whole cloves of garlic. Someone will later remove the whole garlic cloves, chop them very finely and return them to the meat mixture when no one is looking. Technically, you are supposed to discard the cloves, but some folks think the garlic should be left in there, and one of those garlic lovers might just sneak them back in. That someone could very likely be our youngest cast member, a mere bit player in the production, like maybe, me. I'm asking Zizi Thelma how much parsley do you put in, and she says,

"Oh you know, some."

"How much is some?"

"Oh, you know, a good bit for this much meat."

And so, once again I am reminded of one irrefutable fact. Many good cooks, and especially many good Italian cooks, don't measure anything. It's a pinch of this and a dab of that. It's that instinctual thing again, and since Thelma is Nana's eldest daughter, she obviously got that gene that allows you to say "This is the right amount, and if it's not enough I'll add more, and if it's too much that's ok because parsley is good for you anyway."

The meat mixture is now drained and put into a big bowl to cool. And I mean a big bowl. This is the mother of all mixing bowls, only slightly smaller than the baptismal font over at St John's.

My mother has cooked the spinach, drained and cooled it, and is now squeezing it in a piece of linen to get all the water out. She is singing the second stanza of the same song Nana was crooning earlier in the basement.

My Sister Barb is grating cheese and singing with Mom 'cause she's the only one who knows how to harmonize. I must admit they sound pretty good. I hum along under my breath because I don't know the words and, truth be known, couldn't carry a tune if it had two handles on it. I remember thinking now that this is what being Italian is all about. A bunch of people working hard and singing together …... each one happily doing their assigned task so that we may all get together and over-eat.

Zizi Marguerite has finished breaking and beating the eggs, and the whole mess – the meat, spinach, eggs, cheese and parsley go into the baptismal font bowl and this is my cue to start begging and pleading to be allowed to mix up the mixture, just itching to make a big mess. Somebody says (probably Zizi Marguerite who not only let's me get away with murder, but often times, will actually aid and abet me in the particular misdemeanor),

"Okay, let's let Tommy mix the filling." But before I can dive into the task I am marched off to the kitchen sink where I have to wash my hands about nine times. After being inspected and pronounced "clean." I now have the honor to start mixing. It's really a lot of fun to get your hands into a bowl of gooey stuff and squeeze, punch, knead and whatever. The fun feeling lasts about a minute and the realization that this is a lot of work starts to set in and I'm thinking,

"What the hell was I thinking while begging to be allowed to do this?" Finally, when somebody in authority believes the filling to be thoroughly mixed, I am discharged with a nod and a "Nice job." My arms are now hanging down my sides like a pair of soppresata's and I can no longer feel my thumbs. I retreat to the sink to wash the sticky goo off my hands and sit down to rest. But not for long, because Ninja Nana has returned from the basement carrying in her outstretched arms pasta sheet number one. Looking very much like a little Buddha about to make a sacrificial offering of dough to the God *Pane*, she sets the dough down gently onto the kitchen table. Close curtain, end of Act II.

Act III
The Assembly

Trying hard not to get into each other's way, everybody grabs a teaspoon and begins to drop a heaping spoonful of the filling about 2 inches apart all along the dough, in rows. There is much laughing and nudging and bumping into each other at this point. Meanwhile Nana has returned from the basement with a second sheet of dough. When the last dollop of filling is in place, the second sheet of dough is gently lowered onto the first.

We all have a little filling on our fingers, and since Nana is the only one without sticky fingers, she follows along the row, gently pressing the dough between each dab of filling to seal it. She has re-floured her hands for this procedure. I swear, that woman used flour like other more pretentious women use bath talc.

The ravioli must now be cut into little squares which make them well...... ravioli. This is done with a very sharp knife, going down and across each row to make the squares. Moved off to the side, the edges of each square must be pinched with a fork to assure that the little pies will not break open while cooking. This is a very time consuming process considering that it was not uncommon for us to make two hundred ravioli on a given Saturday. Everyone pitches in to make it go faster. Later on, someone invented the ravioli cutter with a little zig-zag edged pastry wheel on a plastic handle, to eliminate the fork–pinching. Someone brings along a round ravioli cutter, with a circular ring of zig-zag teeth and a small wooden knob on top which you press down over the bump in the dough made by the filling, turn it and lift, and voila! These however do not hold together quite as well so you have to be careful when cooking. Often times all three methods would be employed on the same batch, so you might get a plate of ravioli with three squares ones, four round ones, and one which was kind of a triangle sort of thing from the edge of the sheet. No matter—they all taste the same—that is to say, *delicious.*

While everyone is cutting and pinching the ravioli, two of the cast have gone into the dining room and placed a cooking linen cloth over the dining room table. This is where the ravioli will be placed in rows nose-to-nose to dry for a minimum of one hour before cooking. Drying time is not an issue in our case, since we won't be cooking them until tomorrow morning. Since there is not enough room on the dining room table for all the ravioli to be laid out to dry, every available horizontal surface is utilized for this step, including bringing in a sheet of plywood, laying it across two chairs and covering it with linen. The house now totally resembles a pasta factory.

Act IV
The Sauce

Everyone knows the secret to a great pasta dish lies in the preparation of the sauce. The exceptions to this might be in the stuffed pastas—the manicotti, stuffed shells, tortellini, and if course, ravioli, where the pasta is as important to the taste as is the sauce. Almost any Italian you meet will tell you that their grandmother made the world's best spaghetti sauce. I will tell you the same thing. My Nana's sauce was the best I have ever tasted. But to my thinking there are only two secrets to making a great sauce:
   1) Alter the ingredients according to your own taste, and
   2) slow-simmer your sauce for a long, long time.

To tell you the truth, I make a pretty mean spaghetti sauce myself, and a lot of folks have told me it's the best. . . etc. etc. But the fact is, I never make it exactly the same way twice. My grandmother was the same—for one thing, she never measured anything.

"What do I do now, Nana?"

"Mettere in un po di aglio." ("Put in a little bit of garlic.")

"Okay, but how much ?"

" Un colpetto."

"How much is that ?"

"A dab, Tommy, a dab."

"No, I understood what you said, but how much is a dab?"

"It doesn't matter."

Nana thought by translating into English for me I would better understand what "una manciata" (a handful) or "un pizzico" (a pinch) was. The problem wasn't that of English, or Italian for that matter, it was in the third language—that of "cook speak," which is only learned by cooking and figuring out that some things have strong flavors and others are weak. For that reason, you need to experiment with something like tomato sauce to see what you like best.

Another variable on making sauce lies in the fact that everything may not be available all the time. Are tomatoes in season? Can I go out to the garden and get some fresh basil or is there a foot of snow on the ground?

Sometime, I begin my sauce with a canned tomato sauce and paste. Sometimes tomato puree and a can of crushed Roma tomatoes. A mild sauce for my chicken cacciatore. Sometimes I will cook my home-made meatballs in the sauce. I may add chunks of beef roast or spareribs (delicious!) Maybe Italian sausage, peppers, and mushrooms.

So anyway, back to the Ravioli. It's early Sunday morning and Nana is down in the basement kitchen once again, where she has decided to make her sauce because all the burners on the stove upstairs will be needed to cook the ravioli and maybe a vegetable dish. I'm down in the basement helping, her, or at least getting in her way, since that's my job, and she is busy adding un pizzico of this and una po of that, and suddenly she hands me her wooden spoon and says,

"Qui lei mescola!" Hot dang! I get to stir the sauce! This is an important job for a little fart like me. So I climb up onto a stool and stir and stir and stir, taking care not to splash any sauce out of the pot, and I'm wondering,

"Just what foundry did she have this pot forged in? Must have gone up to Pittsburgh to U.S. Steel for this mother!" As I'm stirring, I'm thinking that this is just another Sunday like most others, and there's nothing the least bit unusual about any of this. Nothing unusual about making a few hundred ravioli on Saturday. Everyone has a sauce pot that weighs forty-five pounds empty and every family must surely have an entire second kitchen in the basement. Otherwise, how would they make Sunday dinner? I'm stirring and the lights dim and the curtain closes, signaling the end of Act IV.

Act V
The Cooking of the Pasta

It's now about eleven and I'm waiting for somebody else to come down into the basement to relieve me of my stirring job. Nana forgot to mention that you don't have to stir the sauce constantly; a few turns every couple minutes will do, but being conscientious, I don't want the sauce to burn on my watch. But now I hear people shouting greetings upstairs, which means Zizi's Pauline and Johnny Barberio have arrived, or maybe the Diaz'es, and the arrival of the guests, (Hell, what guests, it's just family) means I have cousins to play with and the hell with the stirring.

Just then Nana miraculously returns. She has a sixth sense when it comes to grandchildren; relieves me of the spoon and tells me to go play. She doesn't have to ask me twice, and I run up the steps to grab Tom and Butch and John Francis and we go out in the backyard to toss a ball around. Dyane will join us too, and that's cool because even though she's just a girl, she can throw a ball as good as any of us guys. Better than most, actually.

Oh, that's right; we were going to cook some pasta. I almost forgot. Not much to say about it, really. You cook ravioli pretty much the same way you cook any pasta. Except in this case, since there are now seventeen of us, we will need more than one pot of boiling water unless we plan to serve them one ravioli at a time. There are three big pots of water boiling on the store. The ravioli are gently dropped into the water and cooked from twelve to fifteen minutes. You don't want the water boiling violently after the ravioli are dropped in like you would, say, spaghetti.

You want just a low boil so the little pies don't break apart while cooking. After about fifteen minutes when the pasta is well cooked you gently remove them with a skimmer or large slotted spoon and place them in a scolodipasta (colander) or as Charlie Giannini's mom called it a "water-go-pasta-stay."

I said at least fifteen minutes because real Italians like their pasta thoroughly cooked, not "al dente'." Al Dente'—wasn't he the trombone player with Guy Lombardo? Anyway cook the ravioli for at least fifteen minutes. If you want crunchy, eat granola.

The drained ravioli are placed on serving platters in layers, each layer interspersed with ladles of Nana's wonderful sauce which was so expertly stirred by the smallest member of the cast.

As the final curtain begins to drop on this particular production, the entire family's seated around both the dining room and kitchen tables. Zizi's Marguerite and Frances have volunteered to sit with us kids in the kitchen, supposedly to keep us in line; yeah, like that's gonna happen. Well, Charlene and Dyane are behaving like two little ladies but Butchie is surreptitiously kicking his brother Tom under the table trying to start something, 'cause that's what he does, and John Francis is doing something goofy, trying to make me laugh (and succeeding, as usual).

In the "main room" my grandfather (Nanu) has taken his place at the head of the table. My mom, Barb, and Zizi Buckie are seated at the front end of the table discussing something important, no doubt. Zizi Pauline and my dad are laughing hysterically at somebody's joke, cause that's what they do (what an easy audience those two)— think anything you do is really funny. Zizi Johnny is smacking his lips and commenting on a particularly hot pepper. Nana and Zizi Thelma are running around like a couple of bees, making sure everybody has too much of everything.

To any outsider, it may seem like a pretty chaotic scene, one that should open a play, not close one, but there is a lot of laughter and love around these dining tables, and the ravioli, are of course, delicious. Just another large Italian family having another run-of-the-mill Sunday dinner, which happened to take a whole day to prepare. May seem like a lot of fuss and bother, but,

" 'Scusa mi, but you see, back in old Napoli,
That's Amore!" *

- From <u>That's Amore,</u> 1953, Capitol Records, written by Harry Warren and Jack Brooks

Grocery Shopping On Saturday Morning
(Pre – Costco)

Before any of the great cooks in our family could begin to concoct one of their many dishes which made up these masterpiece meals, the raw materials (groceries) had to be rounded up at the many local grocery stores in our town. I use the term raw materials because getting fed seemed to be a big production— almost like a factory process. The women didn't just hop in the car and get a loaf of bread and a quart of milk whenever they needed them—oh no! Shopping for groceries was a big part of the assembly line process and had to be carefully planned out like a day in advance. I was more often than not included in the trip, mostly because I was old enough to help carry groceries, and too young (and too ornery) to be trusted by myself at home.

The local newspapers would print the food store ads on Thursday and Friday and my mother, grandmother, and aunts would sit down on Friday evening with the paper and plan the Saturday morning grocery run with a degree of precision, aggression, and detail somewhat akin to the Siege of Bastogne. A separate shopping list was prepared for each of the four or five stores that were the primary targets. Yes, that's right, I said four or five stores. So that's when we would all pile into Zizi T.'s Chevy and hit the road.

Thorofare might have flour on sale—had to go there of course; we went through a twenty-five pound bag of flour in the wink of an eye. A&P might be featuring, let's say, frozen foods, so they naturally had to be the last stop of the campaign. The women referred to the A&P merely as the "Tea Store" (the full name being "The Great Atlantic and Pacific Tea Company"). I'll bet you didn't know that, did you? Well if you did, then you, too, are older than the beautiful hills of West Virginia. I liked the A&P store the best for some reason—I think it might have been the smell of the coffee which was ground fresh right before your eyes. We always got the red bag—Eight O'Clock brand—perk grind (whatever the hell that meant). I always wanted to get the black bag, which I think might have been a dark roast or something, but the women would look at me like I had two heads and say,

"Oh goodness no, Tommy, we don't get *that* kind." Like it was too radical an idea to even warrant consideration. The people in my family were creatures of habit, highly regimented and completely unchangeable. Like it would be the end of the world if just once we got the black bag of coffee. Even at six years of age I wanted to live on the edge.

Between the stops at Thorofare and A&P there were two or three other stores on each shopping spree. Garden Fresh Market always had good produce, which for us meant anything that we didn't grow in our gardens, or that which was out of season. Fruit, for example—being very nutrition conscious, Mom always made sure we always had bananas, oranges, and apples on hand. Being six years old, however my two favorites of the four basic food groups

90

were milk chocolate and dark chocolate.

Kroger's might be the store that had canned goods on sale this week, so naturally we had to make a prolonged stop there. For this we would need two shopping carts, because we never bought a can of corn—we bought a case of corn. And a case of peas, and two cases of green beans —one regular cut and one French cut. *Please* ! Oh, who am I to complain? All I had to do was be there when it was time to eat. By shopping in large quantities, not only did we save a lot of money, but we always had a basement stocked with every imaginable canned good you could think of. Those from the store as well as our own home canned foods. At our house we had one entire room in the basement filled with canned goods. Same thing at Nana's house. I'd be playing down in the basement and Mom would call down to me,

"Tommy, bring up some beans for dinner."

"How many cans, Mom?"

"Two should do it."

"What kind of beans?"

"Green."

"Regular or Shelley ?"

" Regular."

"Straight cut of French?"

"Whichever one you would like."

Oh boy, now I get to take part in the decision making process. Where was this lackadaisical parenting when I wanted to get the black bag of coffee?

There were, of course, many advantages to having a virtual food store in the basement. First of all, there was a wide variety to choose from when preparing meals. Secondly, there was no need to make last minute runs to the store. And probably most important of all, in the event of nuclear attack, our basement could feed a family of four for probably about a year. The fact that the air would probably be unbreathable did not seen to be significant.

But back to the shopping spree. The most interesting stop on the itinerary was always Sam Lopez's store in North View. An Italian specialty store, Sam carried all the goodies that you couldn't get in the regular supermarkets. And once again, quantity was the order of the day. We didn't get a pound of salami, we'd get a whole salami, about twenty inches long, a whole provolone cheese the size of a soccer ball, sometimes two or three. My grandmother would hang them up in the basement to age further. The one in front would be mild, for sandwiches, the last one hanging in the row would be very sharp, for grating onto spaghetti, salads, and soups. We would usually get a whole prosciutto (Italian peppered ham) which my father would slice paper thin. Sometimes a cappricola or a soppresata. Several pounds of black olives, which we "fixed" with olive oil, garlic, pepper, and oregano. Pepperoni—not a stick or two, but a case or two.

Pepperoni was the favorite of us kids—especially my sister. As a little tot, Barbara once threw a tantrum because my father wouldn't let Comari Ciccina go to her house for pepperoni when my grandmother had run out. When the incident was related to me years later (Barb's three years older; I was not yet born at the time), I remember feeling very proud of my sister for standing her ground. It seems I was not the only one to get into trouble for a behavioral faux pas. But we all loved pepperoni. Nana baked pepperoni rolls two or three times a month. We put it on pizza, of course, but we also would eat it with just a piece of bread. When we kids were being finicky, Nana would take slices of pepperoni and put each one atop a bite of her homemade bread. They looked like red tile roofs on little white houses, and she would say,

"This is Zizi Johnny's house and this is cousin Mary's house", etc., until we had eaten every one. Consuming an entire town of pepperoni houses, while listening to one of Nana's stories was a miniature adventure all its own. Eating at Nana's house was always fun.

Back to the shopping—everyone who worked at Lopez's store knew my grandmother, my mother, and my aunts, since they grew up in that neighborhood. An soon as we walked into the store we were greeted by big smiles and hearty hellos. Sam called all the ladies "Honey" or "Sweetie" He was always behind the deli counter cutting meat and would pause to chat with everybody. He had two or three sons and a son-in-law with him back there and they were all learning to cut meat and socialize with the customers just like old Sam. It always took twice as long as it should have to get the shopping done at this store because most of the other customers were old family friends and everybody had to stop to catch up on news from the old neighborhood. Finally, back out to the car with the goods to continue loading down the Chevy, with very different things this time: pepperoni, salami, cheeses, tomato sauce, freshly made ricotta (in metal containers).

Around Christmas time we would get those seasonal items that couldn't be found elsewhere. Things like fresh sweet anise, lupini beans which were later to be soaked in brine and eaten just as a snack. Lupini beans have a hard skin, which after soaking gets soft and pliable. The bean pops out when the outside skin is squeezed between your thumb and forefinger. We kids loved them because we could shoot them at each other like little leguminal missiles. A battle with lupinis was always a hoot, until one of the adults caught us and put a stop to the hostilities.

Also at Christmas time we would always get the fixin's for the Christmas Eve seafood dinner (see Christmas Eve and the Seven Fishes) at Sam's store. The calamari, the cod, whiting and fresh sardines (for frying), the shrimp, and oysters.

The big square trunk of the Chevy is now completely full, with excess bags of groceries overflowing into the back seat. At this point I'm thinking,

"One of these days we're not going to stop buying in time and two or three of us are going to have to take a taxi cab home because there will be no room for us in the car." Somehow we managed to squeeze in, however, with Barb and I sitting on somebody's lap, bags of groceries on the floor between, around, and under half a dozen feet. Not a problem—the front seat is pushed all the way up, Zizi Thelma being a rather diminutive lady and having no problem driving that way. She always drove with her seat pushed forward, anyway, with a couple of seat cushions under her to boot. The Chevy had a three-on-the-column gear shift with a throw that seemed about two feet, causing Zizi T. to always appear to be mad at the car because it took quite an effort to shift gears while depressing the clutch and turning the 1950's size steering wheel all at the same time. She actually enjoyed driving, however, and I used to call her Parnelli Barberio. The way she would peer out the windshield from beneath the top of the steering wheel, I always thought she would have made a pretty decent tank driver along the hedgerows in France.

Back home now and the fun is just beginning, because all this food has to be put away. A quick stop at Zizi Frances' home to drop off a salami, then to our house while Barb, Mom, and I make a few trips across the street toting groceries. Mom stays home to put things away while Barb and I continue the two blocks up the street to Nana's house. Zizi T. parks in the driveway while Barb and I make about a dozen trips down to the cellar where Nana is directing traffic and showing us where to put what. She is making sure we got the Robin Hood flour and not some other brand. No other brand would do. She once sent me back to the store because they were out of Robin Hood and I got Gold Medal instead. When you are the best baker of bread in a town full of great bakers of bread, you don't compromise.
She is very happy with the cheese, but can't help but make a small comment about maybe just a tad too much fat in the

soppresata. Like fat was ever an issue in our family. It's a good thing modern medicine couldn't measure cholesterol in 1957. I'm sure we would have been written up in some medical journal. I can just picture an article in The Healthy Heart Quarterly entitled: "West Virginia Family Averages Cholesterol Count of 325 and Lives to Tell About It."

The groceries all put away, I notice that Nana's spice cabinet is all out of order again (I don't understand how it could be so messy; I just straightened it out last month) so I offer to fix things.

"Nana, do you want me to straighten out this cabinet?"

"Oh, Chickie, would you please? It's hard for me to bend down there to do it myself."

So I begin to rearrange all the four or five thousand little jars, bottles, and tins in nice neat rows—taller in the back, shorter in the front, etc. Ten or so years later as a teenager I overhear Nana telling a story to cousin Mary about how she always had to go into the cabinet after one of my "make-overs" to set things right. It would appear that Nana liked to have her oregano, which she used almost every day, right up front and the cream of tarter, which she used maybe twice a year, in the back row. I remember thinking,

"Why didn't she just tell me all those times and all those years ago?" But I didn't have to wonder why for more than a second or two. Being an expert on child rearing, she never missed an opportunity to build your self esteem. She was not about to deprive me of the good feeling I got from being useful.

"Oh, Tommy that cabinet looks so neat. Tanta Grazie! Tanta Grazie !"

No doubt before I was halfway into the two block walk back home, Nana is sitting on the kitchen floor trying to rescue the rosemary from behind the dried currant extract. Just one of the many reasons I consider my grandmother to be one on the nicest human beings that ever walked this planet.

"Tanta Grazie, Nana, Tanta Grazie!"

Stuffed Pepperss

Ingredients:

1 pound ground beef (or substitute Tofu-Yuck!)
3 large red bell peppers
1 14 oz. can crushed tomatoes
1/3 cup ketchup
   1 4 oz. can mushrooms (pieces and stems)
   1 medium onion, chopped.
   1 cup minute rice
   1 tbsp. olive oil or Smart Balance
   1 tsp. minced garlic
   ½ tsp. ground black pepper
   ½ tsp. dried oregano
   1 small pinch dried basil

Cut peppers in half lengthwise and remove seeds and stems.

Blanch or steam pepper halves for two minutes.

Drain peppers and arrange in oven-safe casserole dish.

In a small saucepan, Boil 1 cup water, add minute rice and Smart Balance and one or two tablespoons of the crushed tomatoes, stir with fork, remove from heat and cover (takes 5 minutes).

Mix the remaining tomatoes, basil, and ketchup in a small bowl. Set aside.

In a large skillet, brown ground beef (or soy) and onion. While browning, add the garlic, black pepper and oregano.

Combine the beef mixture, tomato mixture and rice in a large bowl, saving about 6 tablespoons of the tomato mixture for later.

With a large spoon, stuff the pepper halves with the mixture.

Spoon a tablespoon full of the tomatoes over each pepper half.

Cover with aluminum foil.

Bake for about 50 minutes at 325 degrees.

Blackberry Picking

My father was not a hunter. As a result of this one small fact, I did not become a hunter. I did, however, go deer hunting on three occasions. The first time I did not even see a deer. The second time I saw two deer but could not bring myself to shoot. Whether this was a case of "Buck Fever" or compassion I do not know. The third time I went I did not load my rifle.

My dad and I did spend a lot of time in the woods, however. We went out searching for mushrooms and nuts (hickory nuts, black walnuts, chestnuts). My favorites were the black walnuts. The hickory nuts tasted very good but were too much of a bother to crack and clean. Not that black walnuts were easy. In the hulls, they were almost as big as baseballs. After cutting and peeling away the hulls, black walnut resin stains your hands; you then had to smash the hard shell with a hammer and clean out the nutmeats with a tiny pick. A lot of effort, but they were delicious. My mom would add chopped black walnuts to a home-baked cake or muffins, or use then to top puddings or ice cream..

In the summer we went berry picking. Usually blackberries. No special preparation required. Dressed in a pair of old jeans, a long-sleeved short, and maybe a hat to protect your face from the sun (in my dad's case, to prevent his bald head from sunburn). Equipment required; a bucket in which to carry the berries.

Leaving the house before the sun came up ("Let's get in

the woods before it get's hot, Tommy!"), we would drive to one of about five locations where Dad knew there would be berries. It might be Despard Hill, or the Davisson Run Road. It might be Lost Creek or along the road to Shinnston.

Upon arriving at our destination, Dad would always charge into the woods ahead of me, supposedly to make a path for my five-year-old legs to follow. There was an inherent flaw in this procedure, however. Virtually running to keep up with him, I would invariably get strafed by the branches flying back in my face as Dad blazed a trail through the bushes and brambles. I would usually return from one of these outings looking like I had been pruning roses with my face, and my mother naturally has a comment like,

"What war were you in?", and I reply,

"It's mostly berry juice Mom, not blood." I of course being only five, think it's really neat that I look seriously injured, if only long enough to take a bath and get cleaned up.

Back in the woods, Dad and I had made a contest out of the whole thing, to see who could pick the most berries. Being disadvantaged by not being tall enough to reach the berries at the tops of the bushes, I decide it's reasonable to cheat by every now and then taking a handful of berries out of my dad's pail and putting them in mine.

This doesn't actually fool Dad, but he thinks it's pretty funny and has to tell the whole family that I cheat at berry picking. What he doesn't know, however, is that the biggest challenge for me is to put at least as many blackberries into the pail as I pop into my mouth while picking. He does the same, of course, and Mom can't understand why we aren't hungry for lunch when we get home. It's our little secret as we bring in the harvest with straight faces hiding blue tongues. It's a very good thing to share a secret with your dad when you're five years old. Today it would be called "male bonding". In the fifties it was called "like father like son" or "the apple doesn't fall very far from the tree." Well, neither do the blackberries fall far from the bush.

While we were out picking, Mom has prepared for our return in a very optimistic manner. She has boiled water and sterilized about two cases of canning jars, just in case we hit the mother lode. The reality is that we have gotten enough berries for her to can three or four jars of blackberry jam, another three or four jars of cold-packed whole berries, to open up later, say in January or February for a blackberry pie. Enough berries are held back from canning so that she can make a cobbler, and everyone can have a bowl or two with milk and a little sugar on them, and of course fresh blackberries are absolutely delicious.

I suppose the question must be raised whether a few quarts of berries are really worth all the effort of getting up before the sun to spend an entire morning picking the little devils, getting stuck a hundred or so times by thorns as sharp as four-penny nails. Well, consider this:

It was just such a summer morning when Dad and I had climbed up Despair Hill just as the sun was coming up.

The early morning fog had blanketed the entire landscape and from the crest of the hill all we could see in any direction was a sea of pure white, with an occasional island of green here and there, where the tops of each surrounding hill protruded up from the fog.

On one particular hill about a half mile away, a single blazing ray of sunshine was illuminating a small clearing, in which stood a large buck, a doe, and a small fawn. I remember thinking this was about the most beautiful sight I had ever seen.

It was then that I decided the Lord really had his A game working when he created West By God Virginia, and as a bonus, He planted groups of certain thorny bushes up and down the hillsides which bear small clusters of tiny little fruit as sweet as honey, which, for want of a better name, we call blackberries.

Easy Blackberry Cobbler

1 cup sugar
1 cup all-purpose flour
¾ cup milk
¾ stick butter
1 ¼ teaspoon baking powder
1 ½ cups blackberries (fresh or frozen)

Melt the butter and pour it into a 8" x 8" baking pan.
Add sugar, flour, baking powder and milk.
Stir.
Distribute the blackberries over the top of the mixture.
Bake, uncovered, at 350 for approx. 35 minutes, or until golden brown on top.

Serve warm in dessert bowls with a splash or two of fresh milk.

Peaches, blueberries, cherries, apples, etc. may be substituted for the blackberries.
(I prefer a combination of blackberries and peaches).

The Mountains in Spring

Everyone who has ever been in the Appalachians in the fall of the year will extol the beauty of the forest, fully clothed in its splendor of reds, oranges, and golds. As a kid growing up in the Mountain State, I, too, loved the brilliance of autumn in West Virginia. I have often felt, however, that there was something less often seen and not as fully appreciated.

That something was springtime in the mountains. The big oaks, maples, tulip poplars, birches, and elms are beginning to pop out their first little buds, foretelling the beautiful foliage to come later, which defines the state with its lush greenery of late spring and summer.

The early wildflowers like the trillium come forth in shades of red, pink, purple, yellow, and white. The trillium is a hardy perennial, much like the inhabitants of the mountains themselves. Other wildflowers like buttercups, vallerians, blue-eyed Marys, and a variety of clovers all give their colors to the mountains in the spring.

The dogwoods are among the first trees to color the hillsides with their abundant blooms of deep pink and snow white. These splotches of color are a welcome relief from the otherwise drab vistas of the grey-brown hills all over the state.

Along with the dogwoods, and often before them are the

beautiful redbud trees with their purple and pink flowers. A drive along Route 50 will often yield a spectacular display of redbuds along both sides of the road and higher up on the hillsides as well.

And later come the Rhododendron, which I have always felt was the perfect choice to be our State Flower. The huge blooms of purple, pink, and white that arrive in mid-April to early May signify the glorious beauty that is West Virginia. The deep green leaves that remain throughout the long winter, which, along with the laurels and pines provide a little green to the otherwise barren hillsides. They, too, are a testament to the hardiness of mountaineers.

The rhododendron was my favorite plant, if a small boy can have a favorite plant. Like most everyone else, I suppose I took the wildness and wonder of my home state for granted. True appreciation for nature, like appreciation of friends and family, often come much later in life.

We didn't have a rhododendron bush in our yard. I wish we had. Our neighbors had one, however, and it was a magnificent specimen with huge purple flowers. I was about five years old when I first discovered that you could hunker down under the lower branches of the bush when it started to rain and you could stay dry for about ten or fifteen minutes.

I remember one summer day in particular. A typical afternoon storm was threatening from the west, and I had run out of the house with the sandwich Mom had made me for lunch. It started to rain, of course, and I ducked under the rhododendron for cover. So I'm sitting under there, happily eating my sandwich, when I catch sight of Mom standing on the front porch, hands on her hips, giving me that look that says,

"You silly boy! Come in out of the rain for goodness' sake!"

Moms don't share the belief of small boys that think food always tastes better when eaten outdoors. I remember thinking,

"Everything's okay here. I'm sitting under a rhododendron bush and that makes me a mountaineer. And I'm eating a homemade meatball and peppers sandwich and that makes me Italian."

All things considered, not a bad combination, being an Italian Hillbilly.

A Hot Dog, Please, with Chili & Onions! (hold the Zucchini)!

As you will no doubt discern from the other pages of this book, eating is important to Italians. It has often been joked that they do not eat to live, but they live to eat. And that may, in fact, seem to be true to someone who has not grown up in an environment where the preparation and eating of really good food is important. I have noticed however, that most people who have a real zest for life also enjoy eating well. There are, in fact, many ethnic groups who take pride in their cuisine, and spend a lot of time and effort in making great food. Eating is very important to the Spanish, the French, the Greeks, to name a few. Not so important to the English, or to Scots, however (sorry folks, but you know it to be true, do you not?). As a result of the long-standing Italian tradition of keeping food near the top of the priority list, my family ate well all the time. My mother insisted on regular meals, the whole family sitting down together, good nutritious food from all the food groups, lots of veggies, fruit, etc. Fast food was not on the agenda. It was not called fast food or convenience food back in the Fifties. My dad just called it "Junk" – not junk food, just "junk".

"I don't know why you would want to go eat that junk when your mother has made a perfectly delicious minestra"

It was never considered that what might be perfectly delicious to an adult might not be received the same way by a small child. In our household, we were not afforded the luxury of only eating those dishes we liked. If it was good for you, you were going to eat it. Period. No debate on this issue. This was not often a problem for me, since Mom insisted on a wide variety of food, and I developed a very eclectic taste even as a tot. There were exceptions, of course. Take fish, for example. Being so far from an ocean, all fish in West Virginia in the fifties had to be shipped in frozen and was therefore always "fishy" tasting and smelled like dock water. Neither my sister nor I liked fish. And Barbara would absolutely retch at the mere mention of liver. For me it was anything in the squash family— summer squash, acorn, butternut, etc. I hated the stuff. But I had to eat it.

"Just finish what's on your plate, and that's enough"

We were not allowed to leave the table until we had eaten all that was on our plate. The idea of allowing children to eat only what they like was a concept that was entirely foreign to my mother. You had to sit there until you had eaten every bite.

I remember one night in particular that I decided that I would test my mother's resolve on this issue. She had prepared a side dish of potatoes and zucchini. Yuck! After eating my salad and pork chops, or whatever, I just sat there poking at the zucchini with my fork, moving it around the plate, etc. 6:30 pm: I tried to excuse myself from the table, but my Mom just gave me that "where-do-you-think-you're-going? look", so I settled back down and resumed staring at and playing with the squash. 6:45: Mom and Barbara are doing the dishes . I'm sitting there. 7:00pm: Dad's in the family room reading the newspaper. The kids down on the Fairview Avenue are probably playing football in the street. I can hear them yelling and having fun.

"But Mom, I really don't like it!"

And in her sweetest sing-song voice my mother replies:

"Oh, that's okay, Honey. Don't fret. You don't have to like it; you just have to eat it."

7:30pm: Mom's in the other room, knitting or reading or something. Barb is watching T.V. Sounds like "Father Knows Best" and I'm thinking I'll bet Bud doesn't have to eat zucchini. 8:00pm: I'm holding my ground— sitting there wishing we had a family dog. A family dog will eat anything, and can't tell on you. There isn't even a potted plant in here where I can bury the stuff. Barb and Dad and Mom are now watching "Leave it to Beaver." I know damn well Eddie Haskell wouldn't eat zucchini!" I can see the kitchen clock from my seat at the table and the seconds and minutes are going by way too slow and I'm starting to speculate just how long I have to sit here and stare at this damn squash until Mom decides I've had enough. 8:30 pm: I don't recognize what's on TV in the other room. I must have dozed off. But Dad is laughing so it must be Garry Moore or Red Skelton or… and then I think I must have completely fallen asleep because I look up at the clock and it says 10:20 and there's a groove in the skin on the side of my face where my head must have been resting on the edge of the table, and my mother is asking me if I had a nice nap and I'm thinking she and Dad are probably planning on leaving me here at the table all night and will take turns to check on me and that's when I held my nose and ate the damned zucchini in about four bites, took my plate to the sink and went up to bed. That was the first and last time I ever underestimated my mother's stamina or her ability to stick to her guns where her idea of what constitutes good parenting was involved.

The rule had now been firmly established—you ate everything on your plate, no matter what was on the menu. And, oh yeah, fast food was not on the menu.

By the way, fast food did not come to Clarksburg until the middle sixties. It came in the form of a Burger Chef hamburger joint out in Nutter Fort, a suburb on the southeast side of town. All the old folks (those over thirty) were very disappointed if not downright insulted at the quality of the food.

"The hamburgers are paper-thin. I don't care if it is cheap— it's just junk".

And the worst criticism that could possibly be laid onto a business establishment— "It's just a 'chain'!" In West Virginia, where everyone prided themselves in their work, people put a high valve on individually owned businesses—"Mom & Pop" type places. Anything that was part of a "chain" meant that the product was ordinary, assembly-line type stuff and therefore no good. Besides, to patronize such an establishment was virtually un-American. The raw materials and supplies probably came from some "far-off place". They probably bought the kitchen equipment from Japan.

"I'll bet the ketchup isn't even Heinz. It's just no good. It's a chain". And they said the word as if it were down-right filthy by dragging out the pronunciation".

"It's a chaaaain!"

Somebody must have liked it however; the damn place was always packed with customers. It was not long until we had Burger King's and McDonald's popping up all over the place. But for Barb and I, however, fast food was strictly verboten. We did go out to eat once or twice a week, but always to a sit-down cloths-on-the-tables restaurant. More often than not the restaurant was owned by another Italian family who was my father's "Campari" or my mother's third cousin once removed. Romano's –

Angie Romano, the "Pizza Queen." Fifty years later and I'm still looking for a pizza as good as Angie's. Living in Southern Florida I'm surrounded by New Yorkers that brag about how good the pizza is back home.

"Thin and crispy! Mmm-mm!"

Hey, if I wanted a tortilla I'll go to Pepi's, okay? As soon as you hear somebody talk about a "pie" or a "slice;" you know right away you're gonna be disappointed if you grew up in West Virginia in the fifties and sixties. If you ordered a sausage and mushroom pizza at Angie's, you knew you were going to get a big hunk of sausage and half a mushroom in every bite. And you never had to order extra cheese. They all came with enough cheese to block even the largest artery.

Sometimes we would go to Minard's (nee Minardi's) Spaghetti Inn. Everything on Minard's menu was almost as good as you could make at home. I say "almost" because you *know* they <u>could</u> make it perfect, but why confuse the "snuffies" who comprised at least half of their customers. If you made it perfect, it would probably send their digestive systems into overdrive, being used to baked chicken or a ham sandwich. Also, you have to make a profit. Really good food costs more to make. I understand this. Never disappointed at Minard's. When you factor in you didn't have to prepare it yourselves—you just couldn't beat Minard's Spaghetti Inn.

And then there was Ellis's (Allesio, maybe?) Restaurant. The four Ellis brothers also knew their way around a kitchen. They specialized in both Italian and American cuisine. I would usually get something from the American side of the menu, for a change of pace. The food was excellent, and you could get a choice of about fifty side dishes. There was no "vegetable of the day" They had a dozen veggies to choose from any day you happen to drop in. Sam Ellis would see us pull into the parking lot and yell out a big,

"Hey Tom, how you doin?" My dad and he went way back. And then there was Louie—a great guy, but they never should have let him make the commercials on the radio.

"Hey folks! How ya doin? This is *Looooey!* . Hungry? I'll bet you are. Don't feel like cooking? Why don't you pile into the car and pop up over the hill? Bridgeport Hill. How about some fried chicken? Or maybe a nice steak? Don't want to get dressed up? That's okay. We're very informal. This is Louie speaking and as I always say, *gooodniite!*" I remember thinking,

"What kind of a catch-phrase is "Gooodniiite? Not very original. Who the hell is gonna remember that?" Wait a minute—I'm sitting here fifty years later and I remember! I guess Ol' Louie knew what the hell he was doing, after all.

To a kid the other neat thing about Ellis' was that one of the local radio stations actually broadcasted live from a little booth which sat atop a two-story tower in the parking lot. You could tune your car radio to 1400 and listen to the disc jockey spinning tunes on the radio and watch him (all four sides of the booth were picture windows) at the same time. This gave a young child the feeling of being really connected to what was happening locally, because all your friends on the other side of Bridgeport Hill could only hear the disc jockey on the radio, while you could actually see him as well! This was what passed for ultra high tech in 1958, having no blue tooth or I-phones.

Once in a blue moon (that's hillbilly for not very often) we would drive to a little town called Gassaway to eat at Iaquinto's Restaurant. The thing I remember most about Iaquinto's was that they charcoal grilled their steaks and had a great big cactus growin' in the window. Don't see a lot of cacti in the Mountain State.

So, we did our share of what passed for fine dining in West Virginia, but as I mentioned earlier, we were never allowed to eat what would now be called fast food. There was one exception—Hot Dogs. Not that we ate them that often— maybe once a month—a little more in the summer. Too busy and too hot to cook. My dad was usually the one to think of it :

"Hey kids, how about some hot dogs? " Or he would bring a box of them home with him to surprise us. We loved them and so did he. I say a box because they always gave you a white cardboard box that held about a dozen hot dogs. Each dog was wrapped in wax paper. (Food service paper), actually, not really wax. All the places that made hot dogs followed the same business rules: Make a ton of them. Weiners on the thin side. Buns very ordinary. Mustard. No ketchup unless asked for. "With" meant "with onions." Chili was automatic. If you ordered a hot dog without chili in West Virginia people would look at you funny, not sit next to you in church, and would probably not let their kids play with your kids.

You could get relish if you insisted on it, and maybe a few places had sauerkraut, but this was not a very popular option. Sauerkraut on a hot dog in West Virginia was like electric windows on your car—a few people had them, just to try to impress you, but it never really worked. Not the windows, not the kraut. Chili, on the other hand, to extend the analogy, was like getting a car with brakes. No decision required.

There were several places from which we got hot dogs on a regular basis, but we had our own favorites, of course. Some of the best hot dogs in town came from one or two of the local beer joints. (see Beer Joints, Pinball…), and this was great because the only time I was allowed in a "joint" was to go in with Dad to pick up hot dogs.

Hot dogs were also very inexpensive in the fifties. Usually around 15 cent each. There was one place that actually sold them for a dime if you bought a dozen or more, and we always brought at least a dozen.

Of course, we also made our own at times. In the summer Dad would fire up the charcoal grill and Mom would make the chili sauce in the kitchen. The home-made version usually had big fat "weenies" instead of the skinny store bought kind, so by the time you loaded it down with chili and onions, it was impossible to eat with your hands, and required a paper plate and a fork. The home-made chili sauce is so good that the bun becomes merely a container and the wiener is almost superfluous. Today, when I make hot dogs, I usually eat at least one without the weiner, and I always make enough to have leftovers for a day or two later. Chili is one of those things that is always better as a leftover then hot off the stove. The other thing about West Virginia chili sauce—no beans. Beans just get in the way. A good bowl of chili has to have beans, of course, but the chili sauce that goes on a hot dog does not. It's just ground beef, onions, tomatoes and spices.

Just how the chili dog became the first fast food of choice in West Virginia, out-selling hamburgers and even pizza, is still a mystery to me. It does not make sense.

The frankfurter is German in origin and chili is most certainly from south of the border, and I never saw a Mexican in the Mountain State. But I can tell you this: When folks who grew up in West Virginia come back home for a visit, the first thing they want to do is go get a hot dog. When the Conley's (who lived all over the world), came to visit in the summer, an evening with chili dogs was automatically on the agenda. My Uncle Buddy from Detroit had five kids and brought the whole brood down every summer for a vacation. A great time for me, playing ball and goofing off with my cousins John, Sam, Barbara, Tom, and Joey. Baseball and hot dogs. Special times.

I can remember going into Sissler's with my dad and him ordering three or four dozen hot dogs. Expecting a reaction from the lady behind the counter, much to my surprise she wouldn't even blink an eye, but would just start popping dogs into buns and ladling on the chili. I bet they sold a thousand a day in the summer. Even our relatives from New York all wanted to get chili dogs when they came in—summer or winter. I remember asking my cousin Jimmy Rugino what the big deal was. I mean, can't you get a hot dog in New York? To which he would just wink at me and reply:

"One like this? Forget about it!"

Almost Heaven Hot Dog Sauce

1 lb. ground beef chuck
1 small (8 oz.) can tomato sauce
1 medium onion, chopped
1 tsp. chili powder
1 tsp. minced garlic
½ tsp. crushed red pepper
¼ tsp. ground black pepper
¼ tsp. dried basil
Salt to taste

In a medium saucepan, brown the ground beef along with the onion.

When the onion is translucent, add the remaining ingredients.

Simmer over low heat for about twenty minutes, stirring occasionally (and tasting often, just for the fun of it).

Spoon a couple of tablespoons of the sauce over your favorite hot dog (try to put a little too much on each dog so it will run down your hand when you try to eat it, and you get to lick your fingers. That's how I usually do it).

Saint Christopher

As if growing up as an Italian Hillbilly were not
confusing enough to a young child, we had to be Roman
Catholic as well. Of course, almost all Italians are Roman
Catholic, so this was not unusual in and of itself, but West
Virginia being a predominately protestant state, this just
meant we were members of yet one more minority. In
North Central West Virginia however, we were at least a
fairly large minority. Clarksburg, a city of approximately
thirty thousand residents, had no fewer than eight catholic
churches spread throughout the town. Old traditions
dictated that we have one in every large neighborhood and
one for each of the major European immigrant groups that
had settled in Clarksburg. We had an Irish-Catholic
Church, two Italian-Catholic Churches, the Polish Church,
the Slavic Church, etc.

I never attended a Catholic school, however, and so as a
public school student of the Roman Catholic Faith, I was
required to attend Catechism classes in the summers.
These classes were taught by nuns, of course, with a priest
acting as principal. The sole purpose (no pun intended
here) was to pound as much Catholic ideology and bible
study into our impressionable little minds as was physically
possible on six or eight Saturdays during summer vacation.

The nuns took their mission extremely seriously,
endeavoring to make up for the fact that their little charges
were surrounded by Baptists and Methodists for most of the
year, and no telling what non-catholic ideas had crept into

123

our heads due to a public school education.

Perhaps this thinking was not completely unfounded on their part, for I had already begun to become somewhat of a scientifically minded little boy. I was a great admirer of the physical laws of nature, for example, and believed very strongly in the scientific method (though I did not recognize it in those terms). In other words, I was probably a reincarnation of a Missourian, and you had better show me. Or as my nephew Joey would so aptly put it : "What clinical studies have been done?" The child is uncle to the man.

The nuns however, did not seem to be there to engage in theological debate, their thinking being somewhat narrow-minded in my opinion. Another opinion would have been that they were merely being true to their faith and therefore implacable. They did not seem to appreciate the questions offered up by a small boy. We had secret nicknames for all the nuns, usually inspired by either their appearance or their demeanor.

Sister Mary Mongoose, for example, was of the ilk who presented the information and expected it to be received literally and completely.

About this time in my religious education I was starting to have a problem with the concept of "Limbo", which was the place where unbaptized children went. Having already been baptized myself and soon to be blessed with and subjected to confirmation, I was not concerned with my own welfare, but it did not seen fair to me to leave millions of children lying suspended between heaven, purgatory or whatever, who, through no fault of their own, had not been surrounded by a pack of adults and dunked into a river.

I remember thinking that Limbo was a concept contrived by some early Christian theologian who had no real answer when someone thought to ask, "What happens if a child dies before he can be baptized into the faith?" Limbo seemed to me to be at best a "cop-out" and at worst an unconscionable injustice.

In catechism class, I was always the one who wanted to know if today's lesson is to be taken literally or as merely allegory to prove a moral and therefore useful point. I wanted to differentiate between blind faith in Judeo-Christian tenets and the more philosophical aspects of religion as it relates to the reality of day to day living. This of course always got me into trouble with the catechism establishment and branded me as a possible borderline heretic.

"But Sister Mary Robert, did Jesus really feed the multitude with just five loaves and two fishes, or is it just a story to show us the power of faith? And are these really miracles or merely events that fall outside the parameters of expected outcomes given the ordinary laws of probability?" When shown a picture of a growth in a tree that thousands come to visit and pray to because it resembled the Virgin Mary, I would more often than not see a growth on a tree that short of resembles the Virgin Mary. Hell, I once picked a tomato out of Nana's garden that looked like Jimmy Durante. But did we get all worked-up and call the newspaper and build a shrine around it? No, we cut it up and put it on our salad with dinner that night. Even as a child I knew that if you plant enough tomatoes, sooner of later you will get one that looks like Jimmy Durante. Sister Mary Bob would fold her arms across her chest, shake her head in that sorrowful way and cluck,

"Young man, you have certainly been aptly named, for you are undoubtedly our " Doubting Thomas."

It wasn't that I didn't believe, or didn't want to believe. It's just that I seemed to require a little more proof than the average seven year old mackerel snatcher. And I seemed to be surrounded by well-intentioned adults constantly giving me contradictory information on everything from the origin and nature of the universe to the idea of an Immaculate Conception and virgin birth. Adan and Eve on Saturday morning—formulation of amino acids on Monday afternoon. What is a child to believe? I must say, I did kind of enjoy Nana's little stories about the Saints, however. There is a nice warm and fuzzy feeling a child gets knowing that when he falls asleep at night he is surrounded by a pack of Saints whose sole purpose is to make certain he wakes up in the morning unharmed by the evil forces lurking out there.

Yes, Roman Catholics in general, and Italian Catholics in particular, were very fond of saints. There seemed to be a patron saint for just about everything. The common misconception of many Protestants, however, is that Catholics worship Saints in addition to God. They do not. Saints are important as symbolic personifications of many Christians beliefs, and are highly respected for their good qualities and for the good deeds they committed during their lives on earth—not for any seemingly divine qualities which night put them on a par with the Lord. Many Catholics do, however, use the Saints as go-betweens in the practice of their faith. They might pray to a particular Saint, but if they are actually adhering to true Catholicism, they know the Saint cannot answer a prayer; only God can do that. Subliminal thinking may be that perhaps the saint can pass the prayer along to God in a manner that may enhance the author's chance of the prayer being heard or granted, but every Catholic knows that a prayer goes from the faithful directly to God, not to a Saint.

Another commonly held misconception is that Roman Catholics confess their sin to a priest. They do not. Never have. They confess to God *through* a priest. Most American Catholics no longer go to a formal confession, but confess sins directly to God. This is more efficient, and seems to be a practice borrowed from the Jews, namely elimination of the middle-man.

I always felt nervous and a little silly going to confession as a child. I was in mortal fear of what would happen to me if I forgot a sin I had committed and did not include it in my confession. Would I be struck by lightning while receiving communion on Sunday? Would that ever be embarrassing! Walking up to the altar in front of everyone at mass was scary enough, but a clap a thunder and a bolt of lightning landing on my pumpkin head just as the host touched by outstretched tongue—now that would ruin your whole day!

To protect myself from the problem of omitting a sin in confession, I devised what I thought was a foolproof scheme. To the list of whatever sins I thought I had committed since my last confession, I would simple add one lie. The extra falsehood being the confession itself. Therefore, having included the faulty confession as a sin, I would be forgiven and absolved until next time. This ploy was not to fool God, because even a doubting Thomas knows you can't do that—it was merely to cover my sorry little sinful ass by strictly adhering to the rules made by the church. God will understand. God knows me. He knows my intentions. He made me—imperfect memory and all. Besides, adding just one lie to my confession would only result in a slightly more severe penance—maybe one more "Our Father" and a couple of "Hail Mary's." I can do that standing on my head. Every little Catholic boy learns early in life to pray fast. I could say a Hail Mary in four seconds flat. I always added a couple of Hail Mary's anyway in case the priest was watching and thought I wasn't kneeling there long enough to have said my penance. Priests are pretty old—they may not remember how fast a seven-year-old can pray.

Well, as I said, the old Italians had a patron saint for just about everything. A clap of thunder would cause my Nana to cross herself and proclaim "Santa Barbara!" Saint Francis protected the animals, Saint Anthony, the lost. Saint Jude, I believe, was the patron Saint of non-profit charitable organizations. I made up my own when necessary, like Saint Marmot, the patron saint of small, furry mammals.

The most prominent saint to young boys, however, was Saint Christopher—the patron Saint of the Traveler. We all had Saint Christopher medals which we wore on chains around our neck. A little plastic statue of Christopher adorned the dashboard of every self-respecting Catholic in America—or so it seemed.

Imagine our chagrin when suddenly the Holy Roman Catholic Church announced that Saint Christopher was to be de-canonized. This was the conclusion, no doubt, of some high-and-mighty Ecumenical Council sitting on their holy fat asses somewhere in the Vatican. What was the reason? I was outraged. All these years we had been praying to Saint Christopher, and wearing the medals and all, and from out of the blue came a bombshell. No acceptable explanation was forthcoming. Perhaps too many car-wrecks on the new interstate highway system? The dashboard statues being flung on to the highways lying at the side of the road serving as an omen that God no longer favors Saint Christopher?

In my rage and disgust, I decided that I would not take this lying down. Now nearly twelve years old, I felt like Saint Jean d 'Arc on a mission, and devised a plan to express my revulsion of the Council's decision.

Now Saint John's Church was a large red brick building with a set of wide concrete steps leading up to the main entrance to the sanctuary, which was on the second floor, the first floor being classrooms, offices, storage etc. As you walked up the main steps, the windows on the right side of the first floor were those of the gift shop, where religious icons, rosaries, bibles, etc. could be purchased. The gift shop window always had a sing in it proclaiming something of interest to everyone going into Mass. Something like "Get Your Palms for Palm Sunday 4-06" or "The new Missals are in."

129

I decided to use the gift shop window to express my concern about the de-canonization. So early Sunday Morning, right before the eight o'clock High Mass, I sneaked into the gift shop (the good old days when no church door was ever locked), and posted my own sign in the window replacing the existing one. My sign read,

"Get your Mister Christopher Medals – Half Price!"

I do not know which one of my so-called buddies ran to Father Bandiera screaming, "Tommy Oliveto put the sign in the gift shop window," but surely one of them had, since after mass Father B. is smiling at me and motioning with his index finger in that "come here you angelic little child" way of his and I'm thinking, "Oh no - the jig is up and I'm toast!"

Now Father B. is a very big guy and can cut quite an imposing figure to a scrawny little eleven and a half year old kid.

"A little bird told me that you are the newest sign-maker in our gift shop. Did that little bird lie?"

"I doubt it, Father; it must be a mortal sin to lie to a priest."

"I thought not. Follow me, young man."

So I'm thinking I'm in deep shit now and wondering what punishment he thinks is gonna fit this crime. I rule out self flagellation, since you don't see a lot of that in Clarksburg, but I betcha I'm gonna break the record for the longest penance ever paid and even with my lightning fast four-second Hail Mary's I'm gonna be parked at that rail till All Saints Day—a just dessert, indeed.

But Father B. just hands me a can of Johnsons' Wax and a little tiny rag about half the size of a washcloth and says,

"The pews, Son. They could use a little polishing, don't you think?"

Somewhat relieved at getting off the with mere "hard labor" I'm thinking, "Okay—no big deal. My dad has prepared me well for this." But I'm also thinking that even Dad didn't have a whole darn church for me to polish.

Truth is, after about half way through the first row, Father B. reappears and says, "Looks good, son! No more signs, right?"

"Right, Father."

"Now get out of here—ten o'clock Mass will be starting soon."

So I'm walking home trying to decide what lie to tell Mom as to why I'm late coming home—a lie to your mother being much less severe than a lie to a priest—after all, it's sort of expected, isn't it? Even Wally Cleaver would lay a little white one on Ward and June occasionally.

And I'm thinking, "What good did my act of revolution do me, anyway? Not only did it have no effect on Saint Christopher's de-canonization, but probably prevented me from entering that esteemed group of souls myself. Not that Sainthood was ever really in the cards anyway, me being a "Doubting Thomas" and all.

Beer Joints, Pinball, and Pickled Eggs

One of the most interesting and distinguishing features of the Mountain State's social/commercial side is the roadside eating and drinking establishment—the ubiquitous "Beer Joint"

The appeal of the beer joint is virtually universal among the population. It is enjoyed and frequented by members of every social class, every ethnic group, all age groups, both sexes, every race, creed, and color—almost everyone.

Some are known for their good food, others for the loud juke-box and cold beer. Some are on the fancy side (they are often called "Inns or "Clubs"), but you can never get a room at the "Inns," and don't need to be a member to go into the "Clubs."

The more modestly constructed and furnished beer joints are usually called "Taverns" or "Lunch" (To accent the fact that you can actually get a sandwich there, and not just suck down beers all day). The "Southside Tavern" for example. The name connotes that the place sells mostly beer, has food available and is probably on the south side of something. It could be the south side of town, or just the south side of the street. Sometimes a town or neighborhood will grow unexpectedly in one direction or another, which, given the longevity of a good beer joint, will put the "Southside Tavern" directly into the northwest corner of a particular town.

The name means nothing. The "Valley Inn" for example, stands on route 119 on the top of one of the highest hills in the vicinity—don't even ask. And the names rarely have anything to do with reality. For example, "Lefty's Place" is probably owned by a guy named Robert who is most likely to be right-handed. Likewise, "Sally's Southern Inn" was named for the original owner's dog Sally, who has been in doggie heaven for some forty years now. There are, as previously mentioned, no rooms

135

to let, and the only resemblance to anything southern is the photograph of Robert E. Lee hanging behind the bar.

The beer joint is one of the most important elements of the community's social and economic infrastructure. It is the place where folks go, not only to drink but to catch up on local news, watch ball games, talk-shop, and engage in semi-serious discussions of both politics and religion (supposedly the two subjects not to be discussed in bars, but inevitably the two most commonly discussed, once a few beers have been consumed). You will undoubtedly find two local men engaged in the mandatory "Ford versus Chevy Truck" argument. Frank will be boasting that he now has three hundred thousand miles on his F-150, while Lester claims his Chevy saved his life once by rolling over not once but twice, coming to rest, and he was not even scratched. The truth being that both these trucks served their masters best by finding their way home from the bar after midnight on several occasions without the benefit of even a marginally sober driver.

In addition to food, beverages, and conversation, a good beer joint will have other amusements to occupy your time and test your skills at bar games. Before the days of video games and black-jack machines, there were many other (infinitely more interesting in my humble opinion) diversions. There was of course a pool table, usually in dire need of new felt and slightly leaning to the left or right, depending on how much the building's foundation had settled closer to bedrock, since all beer joints (indeed every edifice) in West Virginia are built on somewhat un-level ground. The bars' regulars will know which way the table leans and adjust their shots accordingly. Don't ever play a local boy for money; he will own the pink slip on your Eldorado before the night is over. The regulars will also know which is the straightest cue among the several in the rack, some of which will bear a striking resemblance to a dog's hind leg. Don't bring your own cue into a bar in West Virginia.

They will laugh at you behind your back (if it's early in the evening) or right to your face (after, say nine-thirty p.m.). Besides—they will beat you anyway, crooked cue or not. You will most likely play eight-ball; nine-ball being for sissies and straight pool requires counting—the ball counters strung on the rusted wire above the table have not been able to slide since before the war. Any war. Shoot pool with Billy Bob at your own peril.

If the room is large enough, there might be a shuffleboard table. A game of horsecollar and a few beers is my idea of a mighty good time. Once again—beware the locals, many of whom actually get better as they get drunk. The newcomers to the game of table shuffleboard will quickly become painfully aware of what a delicate touch is required to get the disk to stop at the desired place. A few games are required to get the feel for it, and just a few beers are required to lose the feel. It takes ten minutes to learn how to play shuffleboard and ten years to learn how to play well. While the shuffleboard table came from the factory perfectly level, in its home in the bar it will probably lean slightly in the opposition direction of the pool table. This might seem contrary to the laws of physics but Sir Isaac never played horsecollar with the Cleavenger Brothers.

Now, I know you're expecting me to say that a lot of the beer joints in West Virginia had a back room where a game of poker might be found. This is not the case. To have a money-stakes game of chance was strictly illegal, and therefore it did not happen. It simply did not exist. Nowhere in the entire state did a beer joint ever have an illegal card game going on. And, while we're on the subject, I have a piece of land for sale in Florida that you really ought to see.

Finally, we come to my personal favorite beer joint game—the pinball machine. Arguably the most beneficial use to which electricity has ever been put, the pinball machine can captivate you. A good machine can grab your attention and feed your hunger for competition as well as, or better than any modern computer game. In fact, the pinball machine was very likely the first practical use of what in a sense, could be called a computer (with apologies to those dedicated limey code breakers of Bletchley Park). Granted, there were no silicon chips or microprocessors, but with all the wires, resistors, capacitors, and magnetos, the guts of a pinball machine was a mechanical and electrical work of art.

And speaking of art, the back glass of the machines were truly magnificent works of art, with vibrant colors and larger-than-life depictions of some of our favorite things—cars, airplanes, motorcycles, fireworks, and women. Yes, they all had to have a picture of a beautiful woman on the front. And they all had to be scantily clad and have very large breasts. I think It was actually dictated by legislation of some kind. Williams, Gottlieb and Bally always seemed to know where to find the big boobs. The unfortunate truth was that whenever you went into the average beer joint, the prettiest girl in the place was on the cover of the pin-ball machine. As if the game itself wasn't exciting enough.

The pinball machine required touch, feel, and skill, as well as an understanding of how each feature was scored. The obvious targets with the bells, lights, and noises were there to sucker you in. The features that you need to hit in order to win a free game or get the highest score were always more subtle and obscured by the bright lights and noise. For example, a "spinner lane" where the ball would cause a little flag to rotate numerous times when the ball struck it, would make a lot of noise and rack up, say, five points for each rotation, while knocking down the ten through ace of spades targets, located in little corners all over the board, might score ten thousand points. The object, of course, is to score a lot of points and this is done through touch (how far back to pull the plunger on a given ball), feel (learning how to "catch" the ball with the flipper to set up your next shot), skill (keeping the ball in play for as long as possible while avoiding a "tilt"), and knowledge (which are my real targets and which are the sucker's "fluff" shots?).

Probably the game that most epitomizes touch and feel is the now-forgotten 25-hole "bingo" machine. These machines held five or more balls, had a plunger to put the ball in play, but no flippers. The solid stainless steel bar in the front of the machine was all the player had to try to manipulate the ball. Through continuous pushing and bumping of the bar with the heels of your hands, the player would finesse the ball into (or away from) a particular hole. There were twenty-five holes arraigned in four or five rows of four to six holes in each row and one hole at the bottom (front) of the machine which brought the ball back to be played again. The object was to maneuver the entire machine by bumping the bar (without tilting), causing the ball to go into the desired object hole (lighting up the corresponding number on the back glass "bingo" card. Three numbers in a row—you will win a new game or two. Four numbers might win you ten games, etc. If you missed the object holes, you tried to avoid all other holes and reach the "out" hole to get the ball back for replay. This was called "skinning it back" or "sneaking home late."

Each game cost only a nickel, but you could put in more nickels for each game to increase the payout (number of games for, say, three numbers in a row), or to give you options to change the configuration of the bingo card. Some options might give you an "extra ball," a much sought after prize for any "pin-ball wizard." These machines were often called "pay-off" machines, because you could turn in your unplayed games at the bar for a nickel apiece. These machines were later outlawed as gambling devices when local legislators finally realized that nobody is going to play 565 games of pinball before closing time.

A fellow could get good very skilled at the payoff machines. Later on, as a freshman in college, I found I could go to one of the local beer joints, and for five dollars I could get two quarts of Stroh's, three hot dogs and a two-dollar roll of nickels, going home three hours later with seven dollars in my pocket. Not bad for a night out. Full stomach (with accompanying indigestion), thirst satisfied (small beer buzz), and a two dollar profit for my efforts. You wonder how they stay in business.

Okay, more than enough about pinball. Let's talk about the beer—after all, it's a Beer Joint. It's mostly about the beer. First of all it has to be cold. *Really* cold. Whether bottles, cans, or draft—got to be cold. The Europeans who settled West Virginia left the idea of drinking beer at room temperature back in Europe—where it belongs. Mountaineers like their beer cold—colder the better. If there's frost on the bottle and you can't even hold it in your hand—that's about right.

What kind of beer was served at these establishments? Good old American Beer. No imports. A West Virginian's idea of imported beer in 1955 was Iron-City—it came from Pittsburgh. But that was okay. After all, Iron-City sponsored the Pirates (on radio), and the Pittsburgh breweries burned West Virginia coal which was shipped up the Mon (Monongahela River). Barge o' coal north, truck o' beer south. Microeconomics at its best—it's a great country!

Besides Iron-City there was Duquesne (also from Pittsburgh—"Have a Duke"), Schmidt's (of Philadelphia), Falls City, Pabst Blue Ribbon, and Blatz (remember the barber shop quartet with the keg singing bass?). And there was, of course, Budweiser and Miller (the old guys never ordered a "Miller"—they called it a "High-Life." Guess it made them feel they were living la dolce vita instead of just wasting away every night in a joint). There was Carling Black Label—West Virginia was one of the few places left where you could actually get your Black Label served

140

by a waitress named Mabel. She didn't look like the babe in the commercials however; she looked more like her great aunt. There was Schlitz, too, (mispronounced "slits" as often as not).

It seemed the most popular beer in central West Virginia at the time, however, was Stroh's. It too was imported (Detroit) and no wonder it was the number one seller locally—after all, it was fire-brewed. Yeah, boy, got that "fire-brewed goodness" goin' on! What the hell does that mean, anyway? Don't you need a fire to brew any kind of beer? Isn't that like saying, "These bisquits are special. They're flour baked!" Anyway, "fire-brewed" or fermented by nuclear fission, whatever—Stroh's was my personal favorite.

Beer drinking wasn't fancy back then. No imports. No green bottles. No microbreweries' seasonal-only brands. Don't even think of putting a wedge of lime in one. Why do you do that anyway? To hide the fact that the beer is made someplace where you're told not to drink the water? Okay, this little wedge of lime will mask the taste of all these little microorganisms. I have a better idea—"Fire-brew" it. Works for me. The only thing I ever saw anyone put in a beer down home was a dash of salt or maybe a couple of ounces of tomato juice—West Virginia's version of the Bloody Mary—don't knock it till you've tried it. Tastes pretty darn good.

The "beer fads" never really made it back home in the fifty's and sixty's. No bock beer. No dark beer. Certainly no "light" beer. Beer wasn't made to be "light." It's supposed to be heavy. Everybody who drank a lot of beer inevitably got a beer-belly. You were supposed to—it's only right. That generation only knew or cared about three kinds of beer. Canned, bottled, or draft. Canned was what you threw into a cooler and took to the pic-nic. Bottles you drank on the back porch, or at the bar. Draft you drank sitting at the bar. A frosty-cold mug with a nice head on it—a little slice of heaven on a hot day. A little hunk of hell the following morning if you had too many slices of heaven the night before.

In college we drank beer mostly in bottles. Quart bottles. "Goin' out for a couple" meant two or three quarts. Drinking beer in quarts had both an upside and a downside. The disadvantage of drinking beer in a quart bottle was that the larger volume meant that in order for the beer to remain cold, you had to drink it pretty fast. The advantage was that in order for the beer to remain cold, you had to drink it pretty fast. Since beer was the only alcoholic beverage sold in most bars (the hard stuff only legal at private clubs), you might wonder if the owner/bartender just might have a bottle of something stronger under the bar for favored customers. And of course the answer is no—never. It was just not possible to ever get a "below the belt" pour from the totally law-abiding tavern. And the place where it was most often not possible was in the aforementioned card room in the back which didn't exist. Something else which wasn't ever available was "hooch" or "white lightnin'". Some of the very best moonshine which doesn't exist in this entire nation doesn't exist specifically in the state of West Virginia.

What kind of people were you likely to find in a West Virginia beer joint? As previously mentioned, nearly all types frequented these taverns. The guys just getting off work, stopping in for a few before going home. Coal miners. Truckers. Doctors. Lawyers. Insurance Agents. Didn't matter. The girls who worked at the office would come in about five pm in twos or threes, but didn't stay late. The "early" crowd. The "late" crowd. The "early during the week but late on Friday and Saturday" crowd. The guys lookin' to get away from the wife for an evening. The ladies lookin' to get away from the old man for an evening (or a lifetime?). Two old geezers at the bar who came too early and stayed too late. These were the same two, who twenty years ago were responsible for carrying on the Ford Truck / Chevy Truck argument, but now it was,

"Arthuritis!—you ain't ever seen arthuritis! Why, my knee gets so big on a rainy day I can't even put my pants on."

"Oh yeah, well how about my prostrate? My doctor says I got the biggest prostrate he's ever seen. Why d'ya think it takes me twenty minutes in the head? 'Cause I can't find everthing?"

And the other thing the older guys would argue about was who had drunk the most beer in their life—an odd thing to brag about, it seems now, given the more interest in and emphasis on one's health and lifestyle. But in those days, drinking was a rite of passage into manhood and many men made the passage so successfully that they took a sense of pride in drinking to excess most of their adult lives ("Never did trust a man who wouldn't have a beer with ya", etc).

Another seemingly mandatory frequenter of the beer joint was the bar-fly—a lady who sat at the bar, sang along with the music on the jukebox, joked right along with the guys (often in the same un-lady-like language). Would get up to dance with any guy who asked (she would often do the asking) and dressed a little on the sleazy side, and wore a little too much makeup to suit all the ladies in the neighborhood who were not themselves bar-flies. These beer joint gals were the same ladies who our parents condescendingly referred to as "floozies."

Every beer joint needed to have an adequate supply of bar-flies to keep up the hopes and expectations of the male patrons. All the guys in the place thought they had a shot at getting lucky, and of course several did (many of whom regretted it later). Picking up someone in a bar in the big city is one thing, but when there are only two bars in town, and you will see be seeing the same folks over and over, a little discretion is advisable. Personally, I have always kinda liked "floozies." They seem to be somewhat interesting characters and often have a more honest approach to life than many of the society ladies who disparage them. These women however, always run the risk of getting a "bad reputation," but on the upside, they will probably not be asked to bake cookies for the church bazaar.

Speaking of cookies, let's discuss the food, briefly—and that's what it usually was in the beer joints of the fifty's and sixty's— Brief. Short order stuff. Hamburgers and Hotdogs mostly, for what was considered a hot meal. The hamburgers were usually okay. Just okay. Almost always greasy, with condiments limited to ketchup, mustard, maybe pickles and onions. The pickles were sweet. The onions were strong. The cheese was standard American slices. Nothing to celebrate. The hotdogs however, were a different story. (see: A Hot Dog, Please...)

Now behind the bar was an assortment of snacks which every good beer joint simply could not do without. Guys drink beer. The munchies set in. There's the Slim-Jims. The beef jerky— tough as leather and very spicy. The jar of Penrose sausages— hot and vinegary with saltines on the side. The snack crackers— "Nabs". There were also "Lantz" and "Toms," but everyone called them all "Nabs." The clubhouse snack bar at the Clarksburg Country Club featured "Toms" brand chips and crackers. As a young child hanging out at the country club where my father was the manager, I thought he was the guy who made the crackers, since his name was Tom. Later I learned this was not the case, however.

Next to the rack of crackers were the potato chips, usually "Toms" again. The little bags of salted peanuts—always stale. Inventory control was pretty much non-existent. The vendor pulled his truck up in the parking lot, came in and filled the gaps in the racks with fresh new product but since there were no "sell by" dates on the packages, the customer was playing a sort of peanut Russian Roulette. So they were almost always stale. But since salt doesn't go bad, you ate them anyway, got thirstier, and drank more beer. That, by the way, is the sole purpose of the cracker-peanut trick anyway, sell more beer.

Also on the back bar was the big wide-mouth jar of pickled eggs, also served with saltines on the side. These can be quite good, actually, and if prepared with the right combination of vinegar and spices, do not get stale. In fact, they get better with age. Don't ever eat more than two, however, because when combined with a gallon or so of beer, can produce more methane than a Doddridge Country gas well.

Next to the snack racks, on the other side of the pretzels (also stale) was the somewhat curious display of such miscellaneous items as pocket combs, nail clippers, pocketknives and "Hav-a-Hank" handkerchiefs. Never saw anyone ever buy any of these items. Not ever. Not even once.

Let's talk a little about the décor of the West Virginia beer joint. There isn't any. Why should there be? Okay, maybe a deer head mounted on the wall. Been there forever. No one knows who killed it or when. At his joint, my Uncle Tony had a two-headed calf in a glass box behind the bar. People would come from miles around just to see it. Okay, maybe three or four miles around anyway. Most pitiable oddity I've ever seen. Tony tried to raise it but the other cows freaked out when it came around, so he butchered it and made scaloppini, had the head stuffed and put behind the bar in a glass box. Looking at that thing will surely make you want a drink, I guess. Whatever works.

What works is having a good crowd of fun lovin' folks, which is the life blood of any decent beer joint, and keeping the good times rolling throughout the evening requires the aforementioned cold beer, some halfway decent food, and of course some lively music to prevent a lull in the activity.

Usually the music came from a Wurlitzer over in the corner, the quadrophonic sound system not having been invented yet. Sometimes a joint might have individual juke-box selection units at each booth or table, so you didn't have to stand at the juke-box to make your choices. This was convenient and since no one knew who played which song, eliminated the snide comment such as "Dammit, Jack, why the hell'd you play that crap?"

The music on the juke-box was always divided into five categories: "Country & Western", "Popular", "Favorites", "Rhythm & Blues" and "Classical" (which no one ever played except by accident (the buttons were very close together). "Popular" included the songs of such artists as Patti Page, Pat Boone, and Frank Sinatra. "Favorites" was Glenn Miller, Guy Lombardo, and miscellaneous "other peoples' favorites." "Rhythm & Blues" was what would later become Rock and Roll (hard & soft) and Soul. We young folk were listening mostly to Rock and Roll and the Motown sound, but not in beer joints. On the Wurlitzer in the R & B category was Bill Haley, Big Bopper, Jerry Lee, Elvis, etc.

The most extensive category was of course "Country & Western" which included not only country music as we define it today, but also bluegrass, folk, and Gospel songs. Bill Monroe in the early afternoon (three guys at the bar). Ernest Tubb and Eddie Arnold around three or four pm (a few more folks filtering in). Roy Acuff, Johnny Cash, Porter Waggoner, Charlie Pride, Tammy Winette, and Loretta (it's gettin' lively now. Saturday nite and the place is filling up.) Chet Atkins, Hank Williams, Dolly Parton, George Jones, Charlie Rich, Willie Nelson, Merle Haggard (It's the shank of the evening). The bar-flies are all wantin' to dance. Conway Twitty on the Wurlitzer. Things go right nice for four or five hours, but now it's gettin' a little late. The rowdies are startin' to fade a bit, their energy waning. Somebody starts a fight; both guys fall down; somebody gets tossed out; fight's over.

146

Good time to go to the men's room. Faron Young – "Hello, walls!"

A few patrons are down in the dumps now because someone played "Blue Eyes Cryin in the Rain" right after "Crazy." The last stragglers are heading out to the parking lot. Going out "Walking after Midnight" with Patsy Cline, her beautiful mournful voice still audible back at the bar. The bar's empty now except for the waitress and bartender.

There are still three cars and a truck in the parking lot. Somebody gave a friend a lift. Somebody got lucky. Everyone makes it home okay. Nobody gets a D.U.I. It's West Virginia. It's 1959. It's a beer joint.

Ficus Giganticus
or
Why you shouldn't plant fig trees in West Virginia

Let me make one thing perfectly clear. I loved my father
dearly. He was a wonderful person—terrific father,
dedicated husband and family man. A kind and gentle soul
with a heart of twenty-four-caret gold. The best intentioned
man I have ever met. But if we speak the whole truth,
well—he could be somewhat stubborn at times. Well, okay,
very stubborn. I should know— one of his genes that were
passed down to me was that little bullheaded bugger that
hangs around on the second to last chromosome. This
particular gene makes it extremely difficult for a person to
see another individual's point of view. In my father's case,
he always recognized two ways to do something, namely
his way and the wrong way.

The following account is just one example of how fathers
and their teenage sons do not have identical priorities.

Upon his discharge from the service for his country, my
father got married and settled into family life in a way that,
to hear others' accounts, made it seem that he was a natural-
born family guy. My father was, as he should have been,
extremely proud of his Italian heritage. One day he
decided that it would be a good idea to carry on an
ancestral tradition which is very common in Italy— that of
growing a fig tree.

149

He then set about to plant a fig tree, not only in our yard but also one each in his parents yard and in my mother's parents yard.

This, on the surface, sounds like a great idea but for one small problem. Fig trees do not grow well in West Virginia. The soil is all wrong, and there is too much rainfall. But the real problem is they cannot survive even a light frost, much less a West Virginia winter.

This conundrum can be resolved in one of 2 ways:

A) Don't plant a fig tree in West Virginia, or

B) Plant one anyway, fertilize it, build a drainage ditch around it, and cover it up completely in the early fall and keep it covered until very late spring.

My dad chose plan B.

This is where I come in. My dad decided as an early inheritance, the honor of covering up the fig trees for winter would be given to the first-born son. I suppose many would think that I should be overwhelmed with joy at the idea that my dad entrusted me with such a great responsibility. Sadly, this was not the case. My feelings at the time were that Saturdays in the fall should be spent playing football or at least listening to the Mountaineers on the radio. If I close my eyes I can still hear Jack Fleming's clear and unashamedly excited voice coming over the air waves.

"It's third and four at the West Virginia thirty-two yard line... here's the snap. Digon fakes the handoff to LaVella and drops back to pass. There's pressure in the pocket. It's a delayed screen pass complete to Lovinski at the 34. Blockers out in front. He's to the 40, the 45, the 50. Breaks a tackle and swings outside. He's got the corner... he's at the 45, the 40, the 35 and forced out of bounds at the Pittsburgh 29 yard line, where it'll be first and ten for the Mountaineers." Simply put, Jack Fleming was the best play-by-play announcer in either football or basketball at any level. All you had to do was close your eyes and you could see the entire game in all its detail. We were indeed blessed to have Jack as the "Voice of the Mountaineers" and it was the least I could do on Saturday to sit by the radio and give him my full attention, not go running around covering fig trees.

Now I know you're probably thinking: "What's the big deal—how long could it take to cover up a fig tree?" Well, let me explain: first of all, the fig tree at my paternal grandmother's house was about twelve to fourteen feet tall with a circumference of about twenty-five feet. I suppose I should be thankful my ancestors were not Brazilian; I'm sure my dad would have me covering up thirty foot tall banana trees. The covering for the trees consisted of a somewhat circular layer of cardboard around the tree from top to bottom. The inside of the cardboard layer was filled with dead leaves to insulate the trunk and branches from the cold air, ice, and snow. To protect the cardboard from moisture, the whole thing had to be covered with canvas tarps which had been soaked in motor oil or creosote or some other foul-smelling goop. Then the canvas had to be wrapped in twine and tied down so the whole thing would stay together.

When completed, the effect was that each of our yards contained what appeared to be a small grain silo (in the middle of town, no less). I remember my friends asking me:

"Tom, what the hell is that big-ass dome in your grandmother's back yard?"

"It's a fig tree."

"Why is it covered?"

"So it won't freeze."

"Does it bear a lot of figs?"

"No."

"Then why bother?"

"It's a tradition."

"It's a tradition" was a stock answer to a lot of questions I had posed to my father while growing up. The annual fig tree conversation went something like this:

"Tommy, the almanac is predicting an early frost this year. I guess we (you) had better cover up the figs the next couple of Saturdays."

"You know, Dad, I been thinking—covering up the figs is

kind of going against nature, don't you think?" An appeal to the nature-lover in my father, a big part of his persona.

"What do you mean?"

"Well, you know—they're not indigenous to the area, and we probably shouldn't be bucking what's natural just to have a fig tree that doesn't hardly bear."

"Look, tomatoes don't grow wild around here either, but I don't hear you complaining about having good tomatoes to eat all year round."

"But Dad, the fig trees don't even have a long enough season to bear much fruit. Why don't we plant an oak?"

"Can't eat acorns! Besides, we had good figs this year."

"How many? Four?"

"Oh, we had more than that. Besides, it's a beautiful tree even if it doesn't bear."

My appreciation for the beauty of trees being much less at age fourteen than it is today, I could see no logic to my father's position, and would have just as soon let all three trees freeze to death.

However, having once again lost the annual fig tree argument, the following Saturday I set about my task of covering the trees. Before I was old enough to drive, my dad would go with me to pick up discarded cardboard boxes. After I got my driver's license I was on my own.

The day began by getting properly attired for the ordeal. Blue jeans and a long sleeved shirt, work shoes and definitely a pair of gloves were required. The leaves of fig trees are covered with a fuzzy covering of cilia, which I happen to be allergic to. Those leaves rubbing up against my bare skin would give me a rash which would itch like the devil.

Cruising the alleyways behind the stores in downtown Clarksburg was how the day started. The object being to find cardboard to cover all three trees. Since we had no truck, this would take several trips in the Pontiac. Sorting through piles of garbage and doing a little dumpster diving for cardboard boxes, I was always a little self-conscious about running into one of my friends during these trash-picking sessions. Looking back on it now, I find it amusing how image-conscious a teenager can be about the most insignificant things. Armed with a utility knife to cut the boxes into pieces, I start the hunt at the department stores, hoping to find some refrigerator boxes. These are the best, of course. Being the largest of all cartons, it will take fewer of them and less work arranging them into the huge cylinder that will be required. The first stop will be at Palace Furniture, then Parson-Souders, and Waltts-Sarter Lear. Hopefully somebody will have just received a shipment of appliances.

After the cardboard has been obtained, the pieces then have to be put together in a house-of-cards kind of structure and tied securely with twine. Oh Yes—I forgot to mention that the three or four miles of twine that is needed has to be untangled, since it has sat in the basement all year, and as we all know, twine and Christmas tree lights find a way to tie themselves into knots when left unattended by humans for long periods of time. The basic cylinder now complete, the inside has to be filled with dead leaves which I have to rake first of course. Since the damn thing is now about fifteen feet tall, I have to carry bushels of leaves up a ladder and dump them into the top opening. I'm now thinking I bet the Seneca's didn't spend this much time building their lodges.

These leaves will provide the much needed insulation throughout the winter and will sit inside where it's warm and moist, and when the thing is opened in the spring will smell very much like dead monkeys.

Next comes the canvas covering. The old tarps have also been sitting down in the basement, folded up into a large pile, much like a stack of bath towels. However, unlike soft, fluffy Cannon towels, they are as stiff as those same dead monkeys, and it is a real treat to try to get them to lay flat against the cardboard. The folds in the canvas give the structure a rough-textured, sort of surreal look, making the whole thing appear somewhat unreal, like it really isn't there in the yard, but is perhaps a hologram hanging there just above the lawn.

Back up on the ladder to put a cardboard and canvas top on the whole thing and securely tie it down in case a tropical hurricane hits West Virginia this January. What a sight that would be— a canvas covered fig tree taken by the wind, soaring over metropolitan Clarksburg. I'm sure that would make the evening news at WBOY.

The back-breaking job finally complete, the trees are now nestled snug and warm in their canvas cardboard cocoons and will most certainly survive the winter. The neighbors are at first curious, but those who have been around a while are now accustomed to seeing these monstrosities in our yards.

All except for Mr. Brown, that is, who has to stand out in the alley behind our house staring at the thing for about an hour shaking his head and thinking lord knows what. Probably complaining to anyone who will listen that having a big round whatever in the yard is going to bring down the property values. He always has a comment or two to make to me, which I respond to with a smile and respectfully submit that I am just trying to save a tree from freezing to death. Mr. Brown is an intolerable prick who hates dogs, children, and life in general, but not necessarily in that order. Pissing off the old fogey for the umpteenth time almost makes the whole job worthwhile.

There is one day, however, during the long winter when the trees actually look kind of neat. That is the day of the first snowfall. If it is a wet and heavy snow, the entire cylinder will be covered, giving the appearance of a NASA missile silo. If it is a dry snow, it will have only a covering of white on top, and it will then look like a giant Dairy Queen treat. From a practical point of view, I must admit that it makes a great target for my bow and arrow. In my Nana's yard, the fig tree served as the football goal post and all extra points had to clear the top of the tree, only to go soaring into Mrs. Townsend's rose bushes.

No matter how nasty the particular winter was, the fig

trees always survived. On a given day in late spring, Dad would suddenly announce,

" Seems like we've had our last frost. Guess it's okay to uncover the figs."

This was of course the herald I had been living for. The upside, however, was that uncovering the figs was only about half the job of covering them. The twine was untied and wrapped into a ball, the canvas tarps neatly folded and returned to the basement and the cardboard merely discarded. The dead fig leaves were easily snapped off the branches and any frozen branch tips were neatly pruned. I amused myself during this task by thinking up new arguments for not covering up the trees next fall, and by composing new snide comments to my father such as:

"Gee, Dad, you worked so hard in the garden all summer, why don't you eat the fig this year."

"Very funny, Mr. Smart Guy."

From the age of about ten to seventeen, I began to think that my name actually was "Mr. Smart Guy."

I was once again feeling cheated because it was now baseball season and uncovering these trees along with work in the garden was assuredly going to prevent me from becoming the Pirates' next first baseman. The fact that I was a so-so fielder and couldn't hit a beach ball with a bed slat didn't seem to matter.

About a week after the uncovering, small buds would

appear on the branches to affirm that we had indeed saved the trees one more year. In about two weeks, beautiful leaves once again covered the trees and in June small buds about the size of a green pea would sprout from a cluster of leaves. These baby figs were the tree's way of teasing us into believing that this year will be the year when we get bushels of fat, sweet figs for our efforts.

I was hoping to accompany this little story with a recipe for stewed figs with cinnamon or sweet figgy pudding, but we never ate any of those things, because figs do not grow in West Virginia, dammit! !

So here is my recipe for Eggplant Parmesan, all the ingredients for which can be grown or bought in West Virginia.

Mellanzane alla Parmigiana (Eggplant Parmesan)

1 large eggplant (peeled)
¾ cup flour, seasoned with salt, pepper, oregano, and granulated garlic
2 eggs (beaten)
¾ cup fine bread crumbs
3 cups tomato sauce
8 ounces shredded mozzarella cheese
1 ½ cups grated parmesan cheese
3 tbls. Olive oil
salt

Cut eggplant into ¼" slices. Lightly salt both sides of each slice. Let set for 20 minutes. Pat dry.

Dip the eggplant into the flour, then the egg, and then the bread crumbs.

Saute the eggplant in the olive oil until golden.

Spoon a layer of the tomato sauce into the bottom of a greased casserole.

Alternate layers of the eggplant, cheese (both kinds), and tomato sauce. Finish the top with sauce and cheese.

Bake at 350 (uncovered) for 30 to 40 minutes.

Christmas Eve and the Seven Fishes

At no time was the Italian heritage of my family more
ed eel, octopus, shrimevident to me as a child than at
Christmas time. The Christmas season in general, and
Christmas Eve in particular. That was the night of La
Vigilia (the Vigil), the wait for the birth of Jesus.

Strictly an Italian tradition (not Roman Catholic, as I
once assumed), La Vigilia was born in southern Italy, more
specifically Calabria and Campagna. Once a time for
fasting, somehow over the course of time the event was
turned around 180 degrees into a celebration, and to
Italians, a celebration became a feast. A fast to a feast.
Works for me. Specifically, it is called "Festa dei Sette
Pesci," The Feast of Seven Fishes. Not celebrated in many
other parts of Italy, the idea found great acceptance among
the Southern Italian familys all over the world, and the
Calabrese who settled in the hills of West Virginia were no
exception. Concocting a meal with seven (or more)
seafood dishes was not an easy task in a land-locked state
like West Virginia, but where there is a will, Italians will
find a way. No amount of effort or sacrifice is too great
for our Lord and Savior, or to be totally honest, our
stomachs. And so with a relish seldom seen we celebrate
La Festa dei Sette Pesci in Clarksburg, West Virginia every
Christmas Eve.

The feast of the seven fishes. "Why seven?", you might
ask. Well, there is apparently no definitive answer to this
one—but there are many theories.

Theory # 1. Let's call it "the creation theory", states that the seven represents the seven days in which God created the world. Very plausible.

Theory # 2, which I personally believe to be the most widely held, is that the seven symbolizes the seven Roman Catholic Sacraments of the Faith.

Theory # 3 points out that the number seven is the most commonly used number in the bible, and attributes enough meaning to that fact to be worthy of a feast.

Theory # 4 is rather more obscure in belief, but insists that the # 7 represents perfection, the Devine. It arrives at this assumption by reminding us that Biblically, the #3 represents the divinity, and the # 4 is the numeral assigned to earth itself. $3 + 4 = 7$; Therefore 7 is the Number which represents the divine on earth, i.e. Jesus Christ. Personally I believe theory # 4 is a bit of a stretch. When I studied religion in catechism class I distinctly remember being told that there would be no math. I believed the 7 sacraments or the 7 days of the week to be more plausible.

I therefore think it reasonable that each Italian family that celebrates Xmas Eve by having a meal of seven fish dishes should be allowed to ascribe whatever meaning they choose to the number seven. Besides, the rules of the seven fishes feast are somewhat loose to begin with. The basic premise is at least 7 fishes. Many families have nine, ten or more dishes. Some families eat twelve fish dishes (for the twelve apostles). Some others may prepare and consume thirteen; not wanting to leave out Christ himself (or the stuffed calamari, for that matter).

If you wish, and have sufficient culinary skills, you could cook fourteen dishes, and attribute that number to the Stations of the Cross. Why not be creative and have twenty-three seafood delicacies at the same meal, one for each Italian who played shortstop for the Yankees? Point is that the number seven is not carved in stone, but it is clear that there must be at least seven.

Okay, so now we know why seven, but why fish? Well, the most commonly held belief is that fish were the only animals ordinarily consumed by humans that were not present at the birth of Christ. Any well-equipped Nativity scene will tell you that the others were all there: cattle, swine, sheep , fowl, and even donkeys and camels. It can be surmised that according to this belief, Italians are allowed to smoke on Christmas Eve, but must refrain from smoking Camels, either filter or non-filter. It is also widely thought that fish is allowed on non-meat fasting days in the Catholic Church for the same reason. I have a feeling however, that the Church's efforts to boost the struggling Italian fishing industry has some part in the equation. Conspiring theories aside, let's talk about the feast itself.

The Italian grandmother always presided over the evening. Everyone wears their Sunday best and meets at grandma's house around four or five in the evening. All the women who can cook are gathered in the kitchen putting the finishing touches on at least seven seafood delights as well as vegetable dishes, a salad or two, pasta, and any number of deserts. Those who cannot be trusted neither with a colander nor spatula are busy setting the table(s), and watching herd on the children, most of whom are only here because attendance is mandatory and couldn't care less for eating fish in any form, much less sitting around a table for two to four hours listening to a bunch of adults discussing how good the baccala is, and " why are we having perch ? Because the smelts just didn't look good this year."

Even adults know that kids just can't sit at a table for four hours without keeling over into their linguine with clam sauce, so the little ones are usually excused to go play. Maybe they'll let us go outside and ride our sleds down the little hill behind the house if it has snowed this Christmas Eve.

The feast begins with somebody saying Grace, and this usually will contain some reference to Christmas, family, and the holiness of the season. Shortly thereafter, a snicker rumbles through the legion of children because one of my cousins has under his breath mumbled an irreverent but humorous version of the grace. Something like "Good food, no meat, good God, let's eat!"

Grace being ended with a resounding "Amen," this is Nana's cue to put down her wooden spoon, tighten up her apron strings, and lead the parade of ladies carrying dishes out from the kitchen, beginning with the antipasto. Now the antipasto could be just about anything. It might be something very simple, like a shrimp cocktail or raw oysters on the half shell. Maybe a relish tray slightly altered to reflect the Christmas season. Instead of celery stalks, there would be sweet anise or fennel (finochio in Italian). Maybe lupini beans in brine added to any ordinary relish tray, served with small pieces of homemade pizza topped with anchovies.

A first course might be fried shrimp or oysters or perhaps fried calamari. The ringlets of squid would be dipped in flour with a little salt, pepper or paprika and deep fried, served with a peppery marinara.

Next would come a serving of soup. It might be clam chowder or lobster bisque. A regular appearance at Nana's house each year would be a very light fish soup. This was usually whiting or cod in a clear broth, seasoned with a few onions or leeks, with homemade croutons sitting on top.

Another staple dish on Christmas eve was *baccala*. Baccala is a salted cod which was bought about a week in advance, and had to be soaked in water, kept in the refrigerator and drained with fresh water added three times a day for four or five days. Nana would serve the same baccala as a casserole, with new potatoes, tomatoes, onions, garlic and fresh basil. When the baccala is brought to the table one of the men will feel obligated to break into a chorus of " C'es la Luna", at which point his wife, mother, or daughter, whoever is sitting closest to him, will slap him on the hands to remind him that this is a religious feast, not a bachelor party.

One of my favorite casserole dishes was the stuffed calamari. My Aunt Thelma was usually the chef on this one. It consisted of flat pieces of the squid, which were rolled into tubes around a stuffing made from bread crumbs, herbs, and parmesan cheese. Arranged in a baking dish and covered with a light tomato sauce and topped with more parmesan. Delicioso!

Served along with the casseroles were the fried fishes. Could be about any fish, but tradition dictates smelts and fried sardines. Before you turn your nose up at the idea of fried sardines, bear in mind these were fresh sardines, about six to seven inches long which are lightly battered and deep fried. Very, very tasty.

Linguine with clam sauce was almost automatic, but any number of dishes might appear. Mussels marinara, oysters Rockefeller, clams origanato, smoked eel, octopus, shrimp fixed scampi style, or langostinos in buttery garlic sauce.

There was usually a seafood salad, such as insalata di mare. In southern Florida we make a pretty mean scungilli, or conch salad.

Intermingled somewhere between the dishes would be a green vegetable or two. It might be escarole and beans, or an Italian traditional dish, brocolirabe (rapini).

The feasting would go on for what seemed like forever to a small child, and would culminate with the dishes being cleared away and the table being replenished with a large bowl of fruit, various unshelled nuts, everyone being supplied with their own nutcracker, and deserts. Perhaps cannoli's. Certainly a lemon meringue pie. A pumpkin pie or a chocolate cake. And cookies. Everyone had been baking Christmas cookies for days on end, and they were arranged on large round trays, one at each end of the table. Probably a dozen or more varieties of homemade cookies.

This of course is what we kids had been waiting for—the cookies. Homemade cookies that for some reason only seemed to appear around the holidays. There were the traditional Italian cookies like gennettes, pizzelles and biscotti. But the bakers in our family were not snobs when it came to baking. There were fresh cream puffs and cherry winks. A German stolen perhaps. Pecan shortbread cookies from the American South. Our family was very eclectic when it came to cookies.

For a seafood lover, the feast of the seven fishes was a gastronomical delight, and Christmas was celebrated with a bang. If you are one of those folks who just don't care for fish or seafood, you might want to call in sick, sneak out for a steak dinner, and go early to midnight Mass for absolution.

One year I decided to eschew the trip home for the holidays, and my mom and dad came to spend Christmas with me in South Florida. I decided I would prepare the seven fishes dinner with a southern twist, for just the three of us. The menu was as follows:

Shrimp cocktail

Oysters Rockefeller

Seafood gumbo

Scungili salad

Broiled yellowtail snapper stuffed with crab meat

Lobster tails in garlic butter

Broccoli cheddar casserole

Pecan pie ala mode

A few minutes before dinner was served, I recounted the dishes and discovered a catastrophe. I had miscounted—there were only six fishes, not seven! Had I counted the yellowtail stuffed with crab as two fishes? They are two fishes, but one dish. Is this legal? Are we going to burn in hell for all eternity, or what? I don't even know how to apply for a Papal Dispensation. Is there a store open on Christmas Eve where I can run out and get some steamers or a swordfish filet?

My mom is trying to convince me that the yellowtail dish counts as two, when my dad, who has not been allowed in the kitchen all evening, suddenly emerges from the pantry with a can of sardines in his hand:

"Hey Tommy, look what I found!"

So Dad has saved the day. We popped open the can of sardines and plunked them right down on the table in a prominent place amidst all the fine china, and that made seven. All's right with the world. Canned sardines in a mustard sauce on a saltine cracker is a perfectly acceptable canape, and completes a perfectly acceptable Feast of the Seven Fishes.

The True Measure of a Person's Worth

Or

*An analysis of character and family values
as defined by the miracle of Pita Impigliata*

the concept…

It has often been suggested that our character and personalities are largely shaped by our upbringing. I believe that this concept is inescapably accurate in almost all cases and in all regards. In my case, I have always thought that being raised by an Italian-American family has been a great boon and blessing. Being raised as a West Virginia Mountaineer also has been of great benefit in establishing good old-fashioned values regarding pride, character, and integrity. Being raised as an Italian Hillbilly, however, is just plain *weird*.

One of the first things you learn in an Italian family, is that food, among other things, is very important. Enjoying food is one of the great celebrations of life. The preparation of meals is not to be regarded as a chore, but rather as one of the sacred rituals of being a human being. The Italian cook will use her skills as a way of showing both her respect and more especially, her love for her family. I have used the feminine pronoun *her*, but it is

171

equally true of the man who chooses to engage in the very loving act of cooking for his loved ones.

I grew up in a family where great tasting food was the norm, and not the occasional event. Looking back, it seems as though every meal was a veritable feast, by the standards of our modern fast-food, eat-and-run society. Sadly, we often take for granted many of the unbelievably delicious and pains-takingly created culinary masterpieces that we were treated to as children. One of these minor miracles is that all-time family favorite, *Pita Impigliata*.

To those of you who may not be familiar with it, *Pita Impigliata* is an old-country gastronomical masterpiece which may be described as a flaky, thinly layered, dough encrusted nut-and raisin log of indescribable wonderment. Basically offered as a dessert or late-night snack, it is the perfect complement to a cup of tea, coffee, after-dinner drink, or espresso. As to its name, a good Italian dictionary defines *Impigliata* as "entangled", and a *Pita* is, simply put, a slang term for a doughy pastry. To call this sweet delight an entangled hunk of dough, however, does not do it justice. When properly made, it has a pleasing home-made appearance and a taste that is (in more modern vernacular) "to die for". The key words here, however, are: "When properly made." More on this little detail later.

The history…

It is not possible, for me at least, to discuss *Pita Impigliata* without also discussing my wonderful grandmother, Teresa Martire Barberio. My "Nana", as we called her, was our particular family's originator of Pita Impigliata, as well as most other truly Italian dishes that were served at our table. She taught her daughters and son how to cook in the true old-world traditions. My own mother, for example, Rosina Luigina Barberio Oliveto, was a fantastic cook who made not only great Italian dishes, but many from other countries as well.

Nana was truly an exceptional cook, taking great care and sparing no effort in making the most delectable concoctions that you should only be so lucky as to sample in one lifetime. A typical Italian *nonna*, she was slight in stature, with a most beautiful, kindly face and long, raven-black hair which she always wore in a bun. Speaking of buns, did I mention that she was somewhat locally famous for her homemade Italian bread, often baked in an outside brick oven? Simply put, if you have never tasted her freshly baked bread, warm from the oven dripping in real butter, then you might as well draw yourself a hot bath, sit down in it and open up a vein, because you have not, nor ever will, truly experience life at its finest.

One of five daughters, plus one son born to Francesco Martire and Michaelina D'Abrose Martire, little Teresa learned to cook and keep house at a very early age.. When her mother died in giving birth to her younger sister, she was but four years old.. It was a hard life in Calabria; Nana's own mother, Michaelina, was an only child whose parents both passed away when she was a very young girl. She was raised by her uncle. By the time she was nine years old, Teresa was caring for her family by cleaning house, washing clothes, and, of course, cooking family meals, as well as baking bread for the whole neighborhood. One neighbor in particular, a friend of her brother Giovanni, lived across the street from the Martire's in San Giovanni in Fiore. The son of Fortunato Barberio and Filomena Scarcelli Barberio, young Francesco teased and flirted with young Teresa by throwing potatoes at her from across the street. This was the man who would later become my Nanu, and would whisk Teresa away from her sisters Maria, Saveria, Luigina, and Maria-Antonia, to marry her and bring her to America.

As I may have mentioned, life in St. Johns, Italy, was indeed somewhat difficult. The family would rent land on the outskirts of town to farm and grow vegetables. They also kept a cow or two, a few pigs, and sheep and goats for the cheese-making. They also had a vineyard where they grew grapes for making wines. My great grandfather was a forest ranger *(Guardia forestale),* so they always had easy access to nuts from the forest; grapes dried in the sun make raisins, add a little farina, herbs, and, see where this is leading? Presto...*Pita Impigliata!*

The ingredients…

The Dough-

8 cups flour
8 eggs, well beaten
½ cup shortening
½ cup Bourbon whiskey
(Can I use *any* kind of whiskey-does it have to be
Bourbon?-
No Dammit! It has to be Bourbon!)
½ cup water
8 tsp. baking powder
1 cup sugar
½ cup olive oil
1 tsp. cinnamon
½ cup warm milk

The Filling-

4 cups raisins
4 cups English Walnuts
1 cup light brown sugar
1 tsp. cinnamon
1 tbl. Orange rind
(all you cooking channel snobs can call this *zest* if you feel
you must)
1 dash oregano

175

(that's right- Oregano! And don't even *think* about leaving it out-OK?)

And don't forget the main ingredient in all of Nana's recipes-*Love*.
Love for your family. Love for your friends. Love for all mankind.

Now it isn't completely clear to me whether the love goes in the dough or in the filling. I think Nana put it in both. Yes, I think to be on the safe side, you should put half your love in each. Let's say you had, oh, say, one and a half cups of love on hand. I would put ¾ cups of love in the dough and ¾ cups in the filling. Yes, that sounds about right.

some more stuff about the concept...

See, here's the thing. All this talk about psychology, with all the band-aid therapists on television talking about self esteem, self worth, love yourself, I'm OK, you're OK, pay it forward, be your own best friend, etc., etc., ad nauseam. Crap! If you are a little low on self esteem, take a look at what others think about you. If people tend to like you, then you probably are an okay sort of bloke. If, on the other hand, people think you're a real shit, chances are, you probably are! If, on your little trek down the road less traveled, you reach a point where you begin to question your worth as a human being, ask yourself the following: "Do I know how to make a good *Pita Impigliata?*"

I learned very early on in life that you should be able to *do* something. I learned this mostly from my father, who always thought that if something was worth doing, it is worth doing *well*. Among the compliments my dad would pay to someone would be something like

"You know, he's a very good bricklayer!" or "He's a very good carpenter" (or doctor, or surgeon, plumber, gardener, whatever). Or: "He's nice to children. "She's very good to her mother" (his ultimate compliment). And intentions counted for everything. On the other hand, if he wanted to point out a totally worthless bastard, he would bring out and dust off one of his favorite sayings, and to provide emphasis, he would say it in Italian:

"Lui non puo` fare un foro in una pizza!" Translation: "He can't even make a hole in a pizza!" Now that, my friends, is a useless individual. I think that figure of speech was the Italian equivalent of the famous West Virginia phrase "Can't find his ass with both hands!"

So, it seemed that certain members of my family would find joy in pointing out how so many other people didn't know how to cook. Or clean a house. Or do the laundry. Especially low on the scale of human worthiness were those who wouldn't even *try*.

"Why, she never cooks! They eat out almost every night!" Personally, I didn't see anything wrong with that— as a matter of fact, I thought it might be kinda nice

177

to eat out every night, if you could go to Ellis's or Minard's, or Iaquinta's, or Jimmie Columbo's. But, I understood the theory. Eating out was a treat. Cooking for your family made you a good person. Simple concept.

Lets make the dough...

The recipe and instructions were graciously provided to me by my Aunt, Filomena "Thelma" Barberio. Zizi Thelma (or "Little Sara Lee" as I like to call her behind her back) is a good cook in her own right, and is known as the "baker" in the family. Her cakes and pies are fantastic. She would always bake a special cake for us kids on our birthday, whatever kind we wanted, and in whatever shape we could think up. A train, a fire truck, whatever. Her chocolate cake is my favorite. Rumor has it she was being considered at one time for her own show on the Food Network, but she failed the screen test. Seems she was not visible behind the counter. Apparently the producers thought it was a bit unnerving to the audience to hear this high-pitched voice giving instructions, while all you could see was two arms over the counter whisking a meringue or something.
Rather unfair, I thought. After all, as long as you could hear the instructions and see the food, what else matters? It's not like anyone ever tuned in to get a good look at Julia Child, for cryin' out loud. Okay, so here's the dough:

In a very large bowl, mix together the dough ingredients in the order listed. Knead to the consistency of a soft dough. It helps if you know a little Italian song to hum or better yet, a prayer to recite while you are kneading the dough. The prayer is not entirely necessary, since you are not looking for the dough to rise, as in good bread making, where a prayer is absolutely mandatory. A little song will do fine. My personal pick for this task would be "La Donna E Mobile", or perhaps Leoncavallo's "Mattinata". Don't worry about omitting the prayer this time, God will reward you for cooking for your family and friends. Maybe not in *this* life however. Remember, virtue is its own reward. As you are working the dough, think positive thoughts about your value as a human being and what a good and kind soul you are to go to all this trouble. If you are having a little trouble getting the "soft dough" consistency (whatever *that* is), Zizi Thelma says it's okay to add a little more milk, warming it first.

When the dough has reached the desired consistency, cover the dough with a moist towel and place it in the refrigerator to cool, to allow for easier rolling. My Nana always had special baking-use only towels for this purpose.

Meanwhile, back at the concept…

In case you have forgotten, we were discussing a person's character, moral fiber, and worthiness. Well, it would seem that in my family, an important determining factor was how much a person would go out of their way to *do for* their loved ones. Like something as ridiculously difficult as making Tortellini from scratch, or adding a wing to the

179

house, or building a gazebo in the back yard, or making *Pita Impigliata.*

Occasionally, one of the women in my family would buy a *Pita Impigliata* at the St. James Church Bazaar, or from the Immaculate Conception Ladies' Auxiliary Bake Sale. Coming home with the goods, they would slice it up, put on a pot of coffee, and we would all sit down to have a piece. This little afternoon "tea" was for the sole purpose of making fun of what a lousy example of Pita this truly was. "Too doughy" and "not enough filling" would be the top two vote-getters on the list of complaints. I didn't even have to taste it, I knew before we even had sampled the wares that they would never pass muster. Once in a blue moon, somebody outside the immediate family would bring over a *Pita Impigliata* that really *was* a good one, and that would really blow everyone's mind. However, being fair and impartial, somebody would eventually say,

"Say, this is a really good *Pita!* It's just like *we* make it." As a small child, I would look at them and wonder,

"Holy Crap! What does this mean? Is the world going to wobble on its axis now, or what?"

Truth is, dear reader, there really are a lot of inferior *Pita Impigliata's* running around loose out there. Made by a bunch of immoral, worthless people (using our conceptual yardstick as a guide). You could be the greatest person in all respects, but well, let's see now, is something lacking? A lady could be of good character, a church-going, law abiding citizen who holds down a full-time job, gives to the poor, is kind to both dogs and children, volunteers for the local hospital cleaning out bedpans, and lectures at the University on Thursday nights on discharged particle acceleration as it relates to thermonuclear stability, but *can she or can she not make a passable Pita Impigliata?*

This basic question is the Reggio di Calabrian version of "Can she bake a cherry pie, Billy Boy, Billy Boy?"

Let's talk a little about some of the really bad versions of this Queen of all nut rolls. Just the other day, my Aunt Maria reminded me about one particular incident. There was this one lady who shall remain nameless (In case St. Peter is watching, and we inadvertently put a damper on her chances of *getting in,* you know) who, I am sad to say is another relative of mine, who made her *Pitas* all doughy, very little filling, and actually substituted *Peanuts* for the English walnuts. *Peanuts,* for goodness sake. Probably voted for Jimmy Carter. And she should know better, too. Born and raised in the same town as my grandmother. I suppose if she had been born in the bayous of Louisiana she would have put cat food in the gumbo. What ever possessed her to use peanuts? I'll tell you what it was- there's frugal, there's fiscally responsible, and there's plain old *Cheap!* That's right, *Cheap!* Look, if the money bothers you, then don't try to make one in the first place. Just go buy a box of Ho-Ho's and be done with it. And this family was not exactly poor, either. Except in character, perhaps. Now, now, be nice. But truth is, when the dear lady passed away, my Nana made a big ole *Pita* and sent it over to her house (I delivered it personally) and her daughter (who couldn't cook her way out of a baking bag) actually commented that our *Pita Impigliata* had "too much filling". *Too much filling,* indeed! Like there *is* such a thing as too much filling. Why, that's like saying, "There's too much cocoa in this chocolate"! Didn't want to admit that we weren't a bunch of cheap bastards like herself, who it was rumored, when she died, she still had the first nickel she ever extorted!

Meanwhile, back in the *Cucina...*

Mix all the filling ingredients in a bowl, using a large spoon.

The dough, having cooled sufficiently in the refrigerator, or the *ice box* as it is still referred to in some of the beautiful hollows of *Almost Heaven*, is ready to be rolled out for our *Pita*. You can make your *Pita* in just about any size, but Zizi Thelma says she likes to make hers about 15" long by 8" to 10" in width. Long and skinny bakes faster than short and fat. With a rolling pin, roll the dough to a thickness of about 1/8".

Nana rolled hers using a long pole about the thickness of a shower rod. I used to love to watch her roll dough. It was like looking over Michelangelo's shoulder while he did the Sistine Chapel Ceiling. Or should I say it was like looking *under* his shoulder? Get it? See, he was on his back, and well…never mind. The point is, Nana really knew her way around a slab of dough. It was a real piece of work the way she made her *Pitas, two-tiered,* the old fashioned way, and that was how she taught her daughters to do it, too.

Some of my best memories of childhood include helping Nana in the kitchen. Not that I was actually of any, help, mind you, I'm sure I was just in the way, if truth be known, but you would never know that from Nana. She was always plum tickled to death to let me "help." When it was time to make *Pita Impigliata*, my job was to crack and chop (yes she let me use a knife, and showed me the right way, too) the walnuts.

analysis...

So here we are, back around the kitchen table, and someone has just come in exclaiming,

"Well I just got back from North View and those dumb ladies at *Our Lady of Perpetual Motion* were selling *Pita Impigliatas* and the proceeds benefit children with unusually large birthmarks, and, well those women do such good works, even if they can't cook..."
So someone puts on a pot of Joe and we sit down and gear-up for a good old fashioned
Raking-somebody-over-the-coals spot of tea.
And then Nana would say,

"L'hanno mostrata soltanto le uva passa!"
Translation: "They only *showed* you the raisins!"
To which Zizi Marguerite would add:

"Questo farebbe un fermaporta buono."

Meaning: "This would make a good doorstop."
All these ladies spoke English, of course, but it always
seemed to add spice to a really good criticism by uttering it
in another language.

So, think about this the next time you are going to drop
by cousin Betty's house with your latest version of
cranberry almond yogurt sesame muffins, or whatever, and
ask yourself, "Can Betty cook?" And if the answer is in the
affirmative, then be assured that the minute you leave,
Betty will be calling all the girls over, and somebody sure
as hell is gonna be puttin' on a pot of coffee at your
expense. If you have self esteem (finally back to some
psychology, you say), you can say, "To hell with Betty and
her guava macadamia turnovers!"

meanwhile, back in the *Cucina*...

So we have our dough rolled out into the rectangle of our
desired dimensions, and to the proper thickness. Next, we
spread the filling mixture over the dough, to just the
thickness of one raisin or walnut piece. This is the easy
part, the filling almost spreads itself. Sprinkle it on using
your hands, or if you can't stand getting your fingers
gooey, then use a soft spatula (if you must).
When all the dough is covered with the filling, start at one
end and roll it up until you reach the other end (single tier
method). Seal the dough, keeping the seal on the bottom,
so it will not show. Tuck the ends together by pinching the

dough with your fingers. Hold the roll together by spearing with toothpicks every 3 to 4 inches. For this purpose, Nana used dried stems of oregano which she grew in her herb garden. I prefer that above toothpicks, it just seems more homey- and original. Carefully take the two ends, and turn them together, making a "wreath". Place on a greased cookie sheet.

Bake at 325 degrees for 1 hour.

Brush the top with honey, if desired, for the last 10 to 15 minutes of baking. This step is optional, totally dependent on personal taste. I for one, think that the extra sweetness is not necessary, I tend to prefer things a little less sweet than most folks. Zizi Marguerite agrees with me—skip the honey.

really deep analysis…

By now you may be thinking to yourself…"Does this guy really think that you can measure a person's worth as a human being by whether or not that person knows how to cook?" To this I answer:

"Of course not! Heaven forbid I should be so shallow! The true measure of your character is whether or not you can cook *well!*" Merely stopping by the store for some hamburger helper will not suffice. You have to suffer, and suffer long for your culinary efforts to be taken seriously. Am I suggesting that a lady who makes biscotti from scratch is a better mother than one who buys hers from Stella D'Oro, hides the bag and serves them to her family on a platter, just because she had to work all day and didn't have time to bake? Yes, of course she is a better mother. At least, according to the Italian Hillbilly book of "Who's Who and Who Ain't Worth Spit!"

Many psychologists will tell you that to develop high self esteem, you should have a mission in life that matter. What better mission than to make a good *Pita Impigliata?* You must also be committed to that mission. I submit the obvious: If you are going to tackle making a *Pita,* you had better be committed to the task. This ain't no Jello Instant Pudding here, honey.

Recognizing that self image is very important to human development, we need to define what a successful personality looks like in a human being. Okay, I think we have done that here. The successful personality looks like this: She's about five feet two, has beautiful olive skin tanned from the sun by working in her garden, wears her hair up in a bun, loves her children and grandchildren and great-grandchildren very much, is always wearing a dress, and puts on her apron first thing in the morning and is still wearing it late into the evening. This successful personality is often seen with her arms wrist-deep in a big bowl of flour, creating a cloud of white dust and an atmosphere of very high self esteem, indeed.

We don't have to look at the latest psycho-babble guru to hit the market to find out what self esteem is all about.

From what I have read, most psychologist and others studying the subject agree that it is very important to be of help to others. This, in turn, makes you feel good about *yourself*. You should try to put a smile on someone else's face every day. Want to put a smile on my face? Bake me a *Pita Impigliata.*

Both of my parents tried to instill in me the desire to always do my best in every undertaking in which I became involved. If you always do your level best, then you will never judge yourself or your efforts unfairly, and will not suffer the guilt or self-punishment that may come from doing less than your best effort. So just exactly what is your best—a bag of double-stuffed Oreos? Or a homemade *Pita Impigliata?* Think about it.

finishing up…

Okay, so the *Pita* is in the oven and you either have or have not brushed it with honey for the last few minutes of baking time. The only thing left to do is to remove it from the oven, and place it on a rack to cool. Once cooled, it can be sliced and served. The unused portion can be stored in the refrigerator for days, nay even weeks (It may however get a little dry if you forget that its in there. It is easy to forget that its there, sometimes, because it is so tasty that a small piece satisfies even the most picky sweet tooth. And there if that tendency to ration yourself on something that you just don't make everyday. There is a solution to this too, however. Go ahead and make one every day. Yep, just quit your job, drop out of therapy and make one every day. No problem.

Now you have conquered the making of one of Italy's culinary delights. Let's talk a minute or two about some optional twists to the basic *Pita*-these have nothing to do with the basic instructions, but are all about appearance and presentation. For example- if you would like to make individual-sized *Pitas*, instead of turning the log into a wreath, simply slice it into 1 ½ inch slices, set them on their sides on a ¼" layer of the leftover dough mixture, and bake in the usual manner (for a little less time), and you have lovely little rosettes to serve to your guests. Personally, I don't care what shape it's in, I just love the stuff. I try not to get too hung up on presentation; leave that to the French. I have never been one to insist that my mashed potatoes need be squeezed out of a pastry bag in the shape of a fleur-de-lis and garnished with rose petals-just smother 'em in some pan gravy and they will find their way to my mouth, believe you me. Did I mention that I was from West Virginia? I like my vits served up *sans* pretension, *s'il vous plait.*

Option #2: Okay now you have rolled out the dough and spread the filling mixture all over it. You start from one end to roll it up as in the basic method, but instead of rolling all the way to the other side, you stop about half way and start rolling again from the other side until the two rolls meet in the middle. The idea here is to put one of the two rolls (the smaller of the two) on top of the larger one. Then you turn the double roll into a wreath and bake in the usual fashion. How do you get one roll smaller than the other, you might ask (And well you might)? When you are rolling out the dough, just make one side a little wider than the other. A sort of lopsided parallelogram, somewhat of a keystone-type rhomboidal shape, that is a rectangle with one long side slightly shorter than its opposite. Just take a knife and trim off a little dough. By doing this, you not only have achieved the more aesthetically appealing two-tiered *Pita Impigliata,* but, since this is a little more difficult, you will probably be automatically propelled into the catgory of *Damn Fine Human Being,* which is a full half-step above *Person of Good Character and High Moral Fiber,* which you get for merely making a good *Pita.*

Both of these methods will assure that you will not be classified in the ladies circle of moral reproach as a person who can't make a hole in a pizza, and therefore not worthy to occupy this same earth as those who indeed, can, make a hole in a pizza and are somehow entitled to and deserving of the air that they breathe.

Now you may be wondering: "Now that I know the only way to acquire a worthwhile character and successful personality is to make someone a *Pita Impigliata,* I'd like to know if this is the *only* way to make one and is this the only recipe?" The answer is as follows: While there may be slight variations in recipes, the one which I have presented here is the one and only true path to enlightenment and self actualization through the culinary arts. And it is, after all, a set of *arts* and not sciences. If it were science, then you could just take a pill or something. Bear in mind, there are out there in life some people who would try to sell you a different recipe (including the so-called old-fashioned version which includes salad oil, nutmeg, and yes, even *cloves,* among other things. Bear in mind, however, that we are not making a cinnamon roll here, or a spiced eggnog—No Sirree, Bob! We are making the real deal. These ill-intentioned individuals are to be regarded as unscrupulous devils incarnate and are no doubt probably communists. Or at the very least fascists. These are the same people who would like to sell you a little horn to wear around your neck to protect you from the evil eye. And as every hillbilly knows, the only effective way to protect you from these sorts of things is by rendering some pork fat with sumac berries and making a poultice.

in conclusion…

On my returning home from my most recent trip "back home", Zizi T. presented me with two large *Pita Impigliatas* which she had baked the previous evening. Here's how good they are: When stopping halfway back to Florida, I checked into a motel for the night in St. Mary's Georgia. Rather than unpack the entire contents of my truck, I brought only a few items into the motel room with me- My shaving kit, a pair of clean underwear and a clean shirt for the next day's drive, my wallet, my cell phone (just in case my cousin John Barberio decided to call me and give me hell about never having my cell phone turned on), my keys, and my *Pita Impigliata*. No, no—you do not leave your *Pita* in the truck overnight where it could be stolen. Some things can be replaced. Others cannot.

I cannot simply run out to the grocery store and buy one—they do not exist. Nor can I order it for dessert at any of a number of great Italian restaurants in South Florida-they do not make it. Why? Because it's a lot of damn work, that's why! And the people who own and cook in these restaurants are obviously not the most highly evolved specimens of truly worthy people of good moral character. And you can't buy one in the Italian deli's either—they don't know how to make it. So, you do not leave your *Pita* in the truck overnight.

Fortunately, being raised by a good family, I had the good sense to bring my treasured *Pita* into the motel with me, and, not only did I arrive home safely the next day with narry a nut or raisin harmed, I was able to enjoy a slice with my morning coffee. And was it delicious! Biting into a slice of *Pita Impigliata* is truly a zen-like experience, unknown to those who have never *been to the mountaintop* of nut-and raisin confections. And, this was not one of those "showed-you-the-raisin" varieties—oh, no! This one was the real deal. The Real McCoy!.

And being from you-know-where, I know a McCoy when I see one!

Printed in Germany
by Amazon Distribution
GmbH, Leipzig